What readers are saying about
Love Yourself Like Your Life Depends On It:

'If you're looking to change your life and you don't know which path to take . . . this little book will open your mind to new possibilities'
*****

'A book for everyone, especially in these confusing times, when sometimes coping with life seems difficult. Highly recommend'
*****

'If you have self belief issues, depression or don't feel great about yourself . . . read this book'
*****

'I would urge anyone who has a deep-seated fear of being unlovable to read Kamal's story . . . it might just change your life'
*****

'This book is a game-changer'
*****

Also by Kamal Ravikant

Rebirth

Live Your Truth

LOVE
YOURSELF
LIKE YOUR
LIFE
DEPENDS
ON IT

KAMAL RAVIKANT

ONE PLACE. MANY STORIES

HQ
An imprint of HarperCollins*Publishers* Ltd
1 London Bridge Street
London SE1 9GF

www.harpercollins.co.uk

HarperCollins*Publishers*
1st Floor, Watermarque Building, Ringsend Road
Dublin 4, Ireland

This edition 2022

4

First published in Great Britain by
HQ, an imprint of HarperCollins*Publishers* Ltd 2020
Published in the United States by HarperOne, an imprint of HarperCollins
Publishers Inc.

A catalogue record for this book is
available from the British Library.

ISBN: 9780008374709

MIX
Paper from
responsible sources
FSC˚ C007454

FSC
www.fsc.org

This book is produced from independently certified FSC™ paper
to ensure responsible forest management.

For more information visit: www.harpercollins.co.uk/green

Printed and Bound in the UK using 100% Renewable
Electricity at CPI Group (UK) Ltd

To James, Kristine, Sajid, Sal, Sydney, and Gideon.
You made this book happen. Thank you.

WHY READ THIS BOOK?

I almost didn't publish *Love Yourself Like Your Life Depends on It*. I was terrified. Here I was, a CEO who'd fallen apart after his company failed, writing a book about how loving himself saved him. I thought I'd be a laughingstock and my career would be finished.

But I stepped through the fears and shared my truth with the world. What happened next changed my life.

The book went viral. Amazing people all over shared it online and on social media. They bought copies for friends and family. They wrote heartfelt reviews. For some, this book literally saved their lives. For others, it was the first time they ever loved themselves.

To think how close I was to giving in to my fears. An important life lesson.

Many readers reached out and showed me how they'd applied it. They asked questions. This taught me that, despite its success, what I'd shared wasn't enough. To create lasting impact, I had to go deeper and share a lot more. I owed it to this book. I owed it to everyone who would read it.

So, seven years after I first put it out, here it is. All the questions I received, resolved. My intention is that by the time you finish, not only will you be committed to loving yourself, you'll know exactly how to do it. And most importantly, how to make it last.

Part I, "The Vow," is the original version, expanded—what I wish someone'd given me when I was at bottom. No fluff, no nonsense. Just simple and practical truth. You can read it and transform your life.

Part II, "The Manual," is new. It lays out the process I've refined over the years to love myself. Then, it shows you how to take it to the next level. Everything here is easy and effective. In a nutshell, it's a step-by-step guide on how to love yourself. Another thing I wish someone had given me.

Part III, "The Lesson," also new, is a record of a time when I fell hard. It bares how I applied everything in this book to heal and, then, rise. You'll see my inner and outer journey, what I did right, and the mistakes I made. Since we often learn best from stories, experiencing my transformation will help you create your own.

I separate my life into before I vowed to love myself and after. I cannot think of a better way to live. Please try it. It works.

PART I

THE VOW

HOW IT STARTED

In December of 2011, I was a participant at Renaissance Weekend in Charleston, SC. Not what you think—no jousting knights or fair maidens. Instead, a conference attended by CEOs from Silicon Valley and New York, Hollywood types from LA, and politicians and their staff from DC. It's like TED, but everyone is assigned to participate in panels or give a talk. The application asked for awards won and recognitions received, and as an example, listed the Nobel Prize. Really.

I have no awards to speak of. Or pedigree. No Goldman Sachs or Morgan Stanley on my business card. When the founder of the event introduced me to the audience at a talk I gave—the topic assigned to me, "If I could do anything . . ."—he said, "Kamal cannot keep still. Whether as an infantry soldier in the US Army or climbing the Himalayas or walking across Spain on an ancient pilgrimage, he's always moving."

He'd done his research. I don't remember the rest, but I remember his last line, "I'm sure he'll have something interesting to share with us."

I had exactly two minutes to stand on a podium and address an audience of scientists, Pentagon officials, politicians, and CEOs—all far more qualified than I to talk about pretty much anything. The speaker before me had been the youngest person to graduate from MIT. Full honors, of course.

It's interesting what goes through your mind at moments like these. Time slows down, yes. But that's almost cliché. There's only the podium and the microphone. You step up. The audience grows blurry, as if out of focus. Clock starts.

And then I knew what to do. I would offer something no one else could. My truth. Something I'd learned purely from my experience, something that saved me. The audience came into focus.

"If I could do anything," I said into the microphone, "I would share the secret of life with the world." Laughter from the audience. "And I just figured it out a few months ago."

For the next two minutes, I spoke about the previous summer, when I'd been very sick, practically on bed rest. The company I'd built from scratch four years ago had failed, I'd just gone through a breakup, and a friend I loved suddenly died.

"To say I was depressed," I said, "would have been a good day."

I told them about the night I was up late, surfing
Facebook, looking at photos of my friend who'd
passed, and I was crying, miserable, missing her. I told
them about waking up next morning, unwilling to
take it anymore, the vow I made, and how it changed
everything. Within days I started to get better. Physically,
emotionally. But what surprised me was that life
got better on its own. Within a month, my life had
transformed. The only constant being the vow I'd made
to myself and how I kept it.

Afterward, and for the rest of the conference, people came
up individually and told me how much what I'd shared
meant to them. One woman told me that sitting in the
audience, listening to me, she'd realized that this was the
reason she came. All I'd done was share a truth I learned.

A month later, a friend was going through a difficult time,
so I quickly wrote up what I'd done that summer and sent
it to him. It helped him a lot. Months after, I shared it in an
email with James Altucher, a dear friend and my favorite
blogger. He replied, offering to feature it as a guest post
on his blog.

Naturally, I refused.

Truth be told, I panicked. Lots of my friends read his blog.
I'm an entrepreneur in Silicon Valley; it's fine to write
about start-ups. But this stuff?

"You have to," James wrote back. "This is the only message that's important."

I shared my fear with him—what would people think? His response, something that I will never forget and will always be grateful for: "I don't do a post now unless I'm worried about what people will think about me."

So I struck a deal with him. I'd kept notes about what I'd learned, the practice, how I'd succeeded and failed. I would put those together in a book and send it over. If he liked it, I'd publish it.

And that's how we ended up here.

WHAT IS THIS ABOUT?

Loving yourself. Same thing your mom told you, same thing self-help books repeat enough times to be cliché. But there is a difference. It's not lip service. It's not a fire-and-forget-type approach. It's something I learned from within myself, something I believe saved me. And more than that, the way I set about to do it. Most of it, simple enough to be idiotic. But in simplicity lies truth. In simplicity lies power.

Starting with the write-up I sent to my friend, this is a collection of thoughts on what I learned, what worked, what didn't. Where I succeed and where I fail daily.

As a wise friend likes to remind me, this is a practice. You don't go to the gym once and consider yourself done. Same here. Meditation is a practice. Working out is a practice. Loving yourself, perhaps the most important of all, is a practice.

The truth is to love yourself with the same intensity you would use to pull yourself up if you were hanging off a cliff with your fingers. As if your life depended upon it. Once you get going, it's not hard to do. Just takes commitment and I'll share how I did it.

It's been transformative for me. I know it will be transformative for you as well.

BEGINNING

I was in a bad way. Miserable out of my mind. There were days when I'd lie in bed, the drapes closed, morning outside sliding into night and back to morning, and I just didn't want to deal. Deal with my thoughts. Deal with being sick. Deal with heartache. Deal with my company tanking. Deal . . . with . . . life.

Here is what saved me.

I'd reached my breaking point. I remember it well. I couldn't take it anymore. I was done. Done with all of this. This misery, this pain, this angst, this being me. I was sick of it, done.

Done. Done. Done.

And in that desperation, I climbed out of bed, staggered over to my desk, opened my notebook, and wrote:

> *This day, I vow to myself to love myself, to treat myself as someone I love truly and deeply—in my thoughts, my actions, the choices I make, the experiences I have, each moment I am conscious, I make the decision I LOVE MYSELF.*

There was nothing left to say. How long it took me to write this, less than a minute. But the intensity, it felt like I was carving words onto paper, through the desk. I'd been disgusted with myself—I could love another, but what about me? From now on, I would focus only on this thought. For me.

How to love myself, I did not know. All I knew was that I'd made a vow—something far greater than a want or desire, an I-wish or a nice-to-have. A vow. I had to go all in or destroy myself trying. There was no middle ground.

In my bedroom, in the darkness, with a city outside that had no idea of the decision that'd been made, I set out to love myself.

The way I did it, it was the simplest thing I could think of. And importantly, something I could do no matter how bad I was feeling. I started telling myself, *I love myself*. A thought I would repeat again and again. First, lying in bed for hours, repeating to myself, *I love myself, I love myself, I love myself, I love myself, I love myself*. . . .

The mind would wander, of course, head down ratholes, but each time I noticed, I'd return to repeating *I love myself, I love myself, I love myself, I love myself* . . . and it continued.

First in bed, then showering, then when online, then when I'd be talking to someone, inside my head, I'd be going, *I love myself, I love myself, I love myself, I love myself*. It became the anchor, the one true thing.

Then, I added anything that could work and if it did, I kept it. If it didn't, I threw it away. Before I knew it, I'd created a simple practice that took loving myself to a whole new level. I was all in. There was no going back.

I got better. My body started healing faster. My state of mind grew lighter. But the thing I never expected or imagined, life got better. But not just better, things happened that were fantastically out of my reach, things I couldn't have dreamt of. It was as if life said, "Finally, you idiot. And let me show you that you made the right decision."

People came into my life, opportunities arose, I found myself using the word *magic* to describe what was happening.

And through it all, I kept repeating to myself, *I love myself, I love myself, I love myself, I love myself*. I kept doing the practice.

In less than a month, I was healthy, I was fit again, I was happy, I was smiling. Amazing people were coming into my life, situations were resolving themselves. And all that time, whether I was at my computer or in a meeting, in my head I'd be telling myself, *I love myself*.

To be honest, in the beginning, I didn't believe that I loved myself. How many of us do? But it didn't matter what I believed. What mattered was doing it and I did it the simplest way I could, by focusing on one thought again and again and again and again until it was more on my mind than not.

Imagine that. Imagine the feeling of catching yourself loving yourself without trying. It's like catching a sunset out of the corner of your eye. It will stop you.

WHY LOVE?

Why not "I like myself"? Or, "I accept myself"? Why oh why oh why does it have to be love?

Here's my theory: If you've ever been a baby, you've experienced love. The mind knows it on a fundamental, even primal level. So, unlike most words, *love* has the ability to slip past the conscious and into the subconscious, where magic happens.

What if you don't believe that you love yourself? Doesn't matter. Your role is to lay down the pathways, brick upon brick, reinforce the connections between the neurons. The mind already has a strong wiring for love. The body knows it as well. It knows that love nurtures, that love is gentle, that love is accepting. It knows that love heals.

Your job is not to do any of these. Your job is purely to love yourself. Truly and deeply. Feel it. Again and again. Make it your single-minded focus. The mind and body will respond automatically. They don't have a choice.

Here's the best part, one that makes me smile as I write this. As you love yourself, life loves you back. I don't think it has a choice either. I can't explain how it works, but I know it to be true.

When you find yourself using the word *magical* to describe your life, you'll know what I'm talking about.

THE PRACTICE

I've tried to break down exactly what I did that worked. And how one can replicate it. Comes down to four things that I will show you how to do:

1. Mental loop
2. A meditation
3. Mirror
4. One question

All four gently return me to self-love. That's the beauty of this practice. It's simple, it's practical, and the results are far greater than you could imagine.

After all, if you loved yourself truly and deeply, would you limit your life to what you previously thought possible? Nope. You'd blow your own socks off.

There is one requirement. A fierce commitment to loving yourself. This, I'm afraid, can't be skipped. What if you don't believe that you love or, heck, even like yourself? Doesn't matter. If you have to build up to it, that's okay. The practice works in a way the mind is designed to function. The mind has no choice but to adapt and respond.

Just remain open to the possibility of loving yourself. The rest is easy.

WINDOW

Darkness is the absence of light. If you remember this, it will change your life. Changed mine. It is this concept that the practice is based on.

Any negative thought is darkness. How do you remove it? Do you fight fear or worry? Do you push or drown away sadness and pain? Doesn't work.

Instead, imagine you're in a dark room and it's bright outside. Your job is to go to the window, pull out a rag, and start cleaning. Just clean. And soon enough, light enters naturally, taking the darkness away.

It's that simple. Each time the mind shifts to darkness—fear, worry, pain, you name it—when you notice, clean the window. Light will flow in.

I. MENTAL LOOP

I sit at my desk. San Francisco sparkles through the large bedroom windows. A Coca-Cola sign blinks off, then rebuilds itself, one letter at a time. I see cars on Market Street, red taillights. The famous tower over Twin Peaks is swallowed up by the night, hidden by fog.

If you were to open up my head at this moment and peer within, you'd find yourself asking with a thick southern drawl, "Does this boy not have an imagination?"

There is only one thought running through my head: *I love myself. I love myself. I love myself.*

For days, ever since I made the vow, this has been my only focus. Sometimes as a whisper, sometimes silent. When I brush my teeth, mumbling. In the shower, loud. Nonstop. "I love myself, I love myself, I love myself."

I have nothing to lose. This is all there is. I love myself, I love myself, I don't give a damn about anything else, I love myself.

I once heard someone explain thoughts as this: we, as human beings, think that we're thinking. Not true. Most of the time, we're remembering. We're reliving memories.

We're running familiar patterns and loops in our head. For happiness, for procrastination, for sadness. Fears, hopes, dreams, desires. We have loops for everything.

We keep replaying the loops and they, in turn, trigger feelings. It's automatic to the point where we believe that we have no choice. But that is far from the truth.

Imagine a thought loop as this: a pathway laid down by constant use. Like a groove in rock created by water. Enough time, enough intensity, and you've got a river.

If you had a thought once, it has no power over you. Repeat it again and again, especially with emotional intensity—feeling it—and over time, you're creating the grooves, the mental river. Then it controls you.

And that is why a focused mental loop is the solution. Take this one thought, *I love myself*. Add emotional intensity because it deepens the groove faster than anything. Feel the thought. Run it again and again. Feel it. Run it. Whether you believe it or not doesn't matter, just focus on this one thought. Make it your truth.

The goal here is to create a groove deeper than the ones laid down over the years—the ones that create disempowering feelings. They took time as well. Some we've had since childhood.

Which is why this requires a focused commitment. Why it must be a practice. Forget demolishing the grooves of the past. What you're creating is a new groove so deep, so powerful, that your thoughts will automatically flow down this one.

It takes time, sure. Took me a month to go from misery to magic. But you will notice changes, shifts in your feelings, beautiful happenings in your life. Expect them. There'll be more and more until one day, you'll be walking outside in the sunshine, feeling good, loving life and life loving you back, and you'll stop and realize that it's now your natural state.

Can you imagine a better way to be?

2. A MEDITATION

Even if you don't do anything else, please do this. It will make a difference.

Each day, I meditate for seven minutes. Why seven minutes? Because I put on a piece of music that I like, one that is soothing and calm, piano and flute, one that I associate good feelings with, and it happens to be seven minutes long.

I sit with my back against a wall, put on my headphones, listen to the music, and imagine galaxies and stars and the Universe above, and I imagine all the light from space flowing into my head and down into my body, going wherever it needs to go.

I breathe slowly, naturally. As I inhale, I think, *I love myself*. Then I exhale and let out whatever the response in my mind and body is, whether there is one or not. That's it. Simple.

Inhale: I love myself.

Exhale: Breathe out what comes up.

Inhale, exhale, inhale, exhale. Natural. The music flows.

The mind wanders, that's its nature. Each time it does, I just notice where I am in the breath. If inhaling, I shift to *I love myself.* If exhaling, I shift to letting out whatever is in the mind and body.

Occasionally, I shift my attention to the light flowing in from above. Sometimes, I do that each time I inhale. Before I know it, the seven minutes are up and the meditation is over.

There is something to this, the thought of light flowing into my head from galaxies and stars. The concept of light itself. Just like love, the subconscious has a positive association with light. Plants grow toward the light. As human beings, we crave light. We find sunrises and sunsets and a bright moon beautiful and calming.

Once again, there's no need to consciously create healing or anything positive. The subconscious takes care of it. All I have to do is give it the image—in this case, light; give it the thought—in this case, loving myself. It does the rest.

This is an intense practice because it is focused. But does it feel intense? No, quite peaceful, actually. I think that's what real emotional intensity is, one that creates peace and love and growth.

Instructions

Step 1: Put on music. Something soothing, gentle, preferably instrumental. A piece that makes you feel good.

Step 2: Sit with your back against a wall or window. Cross your legs or stretch them out, whatever feels natural.

Step 3: Close your eyes. Smile slowly. Imagine a beam of light pouring into your head from above.

Step 4: Breathe in, say to yourself in your mind, *I love myself.* Slowly. Be gentle with yourself.

Step 5: Breathe out and along with it, anything that arises. Any thoughts, emotions, feelings, memories, fears, hopes, desires. Or nothing. Breathe it out. No judgment, no attachment to anything. Be kind to yourself.

Step 6: Repeat 4 and 5 until the music ends.

(When your attention wanders, notice it and smile. Smile at it as if it's a child doing what a child does. And with that smile, return to your breath. Step 4, step 5. Mind wanders, notice, smile kindly, return to step 4, step 5.)

Step 7: When the music ends, open your eyes slowly. Smile. Do it from the inside out. This is your time. This is purely yours.

Why music? Since I listen to the same piece each time, it now acts as an anchor, easily pulling me into a meditative state. A crutch perhaps, but a nice one.

Do this meditation consistently. You will notice the magic that occurs.

3. MIRROR

This one, I'm a little scared to share. People will think I've lost it. But it is powerful.

Step 1: Set a timer for five minutes.

Step 2: Stand in front of a mirror, nose a few inches away. Relax. Breathe.

Step 3: Look into your eyes. It sometimes helps to focus on just one. If so, try your left eye. Breathe slowly, naturally, until you develop a rhythm.

Step 4: Looking into your eyes, say, "I love myself." Whether you believe it that moment or not isn't important. What's important is you saying it to yourself, looking into your eyes, where there is no escape from the truth. And ultimately, the truth is loving yourself.

Step 5: Repeat "I love myself" gently, pausing occasionally to watch your eyes.

When the five minutes are up, smile. You've just communicated the truth to yourself in a deep, visceral way. In a way the mind cannot escape.

If anyone ever looked in your eyes, knowing that you loved them, this is what they saw. Give yourself the same gift.

4. ONE QUESTION

It's easy to say "I love myself" while locked inside my apartment, recovering from being sick. Tougher when I'm back to the land of the living, interacting with people who have their own issues and mental loops.

That is where the question came from. In dealing with others and reacting to their negative emotions with my own, I found myself asking this question:

If I loved myself truly and deeply, would I let myself experience this?

The answer, always, was a no.

It worked beautifully. Because I'd been working on the mental loop, the step after no was clear. Rather than solving the emotion or trying not to feel it, I would just return to the one true thing in my head, *I love myself, I love myself, I love myself*.

This question is deceptively simple in its power. It shifts your focus from wherever you are—whether it's anger or pain or fear, any form of darkness—to where you want to be. And that is love. Your mind and life have no choice but to follow.

THOUGHT

If we are made of atoms and molecules, and they in turn from smaller particles that are empty space and energy, then what are we?

Are we our thoughts?

Ever catch your mind in a mental loop, replaying some old story, an old hurt, the same pattern? Who are you? The thought or the observer of the thought?

If you're the observer, then what is the thought?

Or are you a thought observing another thought?

Perhaps we're just biochemical storms within synaptic connections in a brain that evolved over millions of years. Or maybe there is an observer, a deeper self. No proof either way.

I'm fine with not knowing. I enjoy thinking about it, but mainly to remind myself that ultimately, everything is theory. I care about what works. What creates magic in my life.

This I know: the mind, left to itself, repeats the same stories, the same loops. Mostly ones that don't serve us. So what's practical, what's transformative, is to consciously choose a thought. Then practice it again and again. With emotion, with feeling, with acceptance.

Lay down the synaptic pathways until the mind starts playing it automatically. Do this with enough intensity over time and the mind will have no choice. That's how it operates. Where do you think your original loops came from?

The goal, if there is one, is to practice until the thought you chose becomes the primary loop. Until it becomes the filter through which you view life. Then practice some more.

Sounds like work. Perhaps. But the nature of mind is thought. Choose one that transforms you, makes your life zing. The one I found, *I love myself*, is the most powerful one I know. You might discover another. Regardless, please do it.

It is worth it.

MEMORY

Memory is not set in stone. Any neuroscientist will tell you that. The more you remember something, especially if it's emotionally charged, the more you will reinforce the pathways connecting the neurons. Simply put, the more you think about it, the more you feel it, the stronger the memory.

Here's the interesting part. It's not just the act of recall that strengthens a memory; another factor shapes and even changes it—the state of mind you are in when remembering something.

The implications of this are transformative.

Take a random experience, a relationship that ended years ago. Consciously recall it when you're miserable. You'll find yourself focusing on the negative parts, and those will grow stronger in memory.

Conversely, same exact experience, but recall when you're happy. Notice the change?

It's still the same experience, it's still your mind. But the filter is different. And the filter shifts the focus, which subtly changes the memory. More importantly, it changes how the memory makes you feel, the power it has over you.

There's a solution here, a powerful one.

If a painful memory arises, don't fight it or try to push it away—you're in quicksand. Struggle reinforces pain. Instead, go to love. Love for yourself. Feel it. If you have to fake it, fine. It'll become real eventually. Feel the love for yourself as the memory ebbs and flows. That will take the power away.

And, even more importantly, it will shift the wiring of the memory. Do it again and again. Love. Rewire. Love. Rewire. It's your mind. You can do whatever you want.

LIGHT SWITCHES

Richard Bandler, cocreator of NLP, became known early in his career as someone who could cure schizophrenics within hours. He started getting called by doctors and patients' families to go to mental institutions, to work with the worst cases, the ones everyone had given up on.

One of his favorite stories is about an executive who started hallucinating snakes. No one could convince him otherwise. He was committed, received treatment, no luck. So he was strapped to his bed—not very empowering when you believe snakes are crawling all over you—in the mental hospital and chalked off as one of the incurable ones.

By the time Bandler met him, he was in bad shape. To figure out what to do, Bandler went for a walk in town. He needed to snap this guy back to reality. He passed a pet store and noticed a barrel full of rubber snakes on the curb. He went inside, asked the man behind the counter if he could rent the entire barrel for a few hours.

"They're for sale," the man said. "I don't rent the whole barrel."

"I need them," Bandler said, "all. But only for a few hours."

"Why?"

"I'm going to cure schizophrenia," Bandler said.

"Cool," the man said.

Bandler chalks it up to the fact that since the store owner wasn't a doctor, his mind was open to cures that were out of the norm. Turns out he also had a few well-trained snakes—two cobras and one giant python that loved wrapping herself around humans. Perfect.

The store owner and Bandler returned to the mental hospital, bags full of rubber snakes and three real ones, went to the shower where the patient bathed, and covered the place with them. The live cobras, he put extra close to where the patient would be. The python, right above where he'd position the wheelchair. Finished, he surveyed his work.

It reminded him of the scene from *Raiders of the Lost Ark* where Indiana Jones descends into a chamber full of writhing snakes. Enough to scare anyone, let alone a person with heightened snake phobia.

Keep in mind, Bandler once cured a guy who thought he was Jesus by bringing three muscular football players dressed as Roman centurions and wood for a life-size cross into his hospital room. Then, he proceeded to nail the cross together, pausing occasionally to measure the guy as the centurions held him down. By the time they were ready for the crucifixion, the man was convinced he wasn't Jesus. Even after the drama had passed, the cure stuck.

The snake owner and doctor stood behind the one-way glass to the shower. Bandler brought the man in, strapped tight in his wheelchair. The moment the man saw the snakes, he started screaming, "Snakes!"

It was a terrible sound, Bandler says, from the very depths of the man, carrying throughout the hospital, "Snaaaaaakes!" But he positioned the man right where he could see the cobras in front and the python dangling above. Then he left and shut the door behind him.

The man screamed and screamed. Bandler waited. Finally, he went in. The man saw him, was about to scream, but Bandler cut him off.

"Snakes snakes, yes I know," Bandler said. "Tell me which ones are real and which ones aren't, and I'll wheel you out. Otherwise, I'm leaving you in here." Then he turned to go.

"Rubber snakes," the man said, motioning to the ground with his head. "Hallucinated snakes." He motioned around. Then, eyes up at the python dangling a few feet above, dropping closer, "Real snake!"

This caught Bandler off guard. The man, when put to the test, was not only lucid enough to distinguish real from hallucinated, he could even tell which ones were rubber—something Bandler had a hard time telling, given how realistic they were.

He wheeled the man out and asked him how he could tell hallucinated versus real.

"Easy," the man said, "hallucinated snakes are see-through."

The man had known all along. Reality was solid, hallucinations were see-through. But his fear was so intense, he'd lost touch with reality. Bandler taught the man to focus on the difference between reality and hallucinated see-through snakes and the man was cured. He still saw hallucinated snakes occasionally, but knew that they were not real. The power they had over him was gone.

Fighting fear doesn't work. It just drags us in closer. One has to focus on what is real. On the truth. When in darkness, don't fight it. You can't win. Just find the nearest switch, turn on the light.

James Altucher, in one of his best blog posts, talks about how he stops negative thoughts in their tracks with a simple mind trick. "Not useful," he tells himself. It's a switch, a breaker of sorts, shifts the pattern of the fear.

In the last book of the Hunger Games trilogy, one of the main characters has been tortured by the Capitol, his memories altered so that he can't distinguish between actual and implanted memories. His friends come up with a simple exercise. They tell him memories they know to be true, then ask, "real or not real?" Slowly, he learns to distinguish real from not real until his mind adapts and he realizes that not-real memories have a certain shininess to them. And when in doubt, he returns to the practice: real or not real.

Fear, when used properly, is a useful tool. It serves us well when near a blazing inferno or standing at the edge of a cliff. But outside of this, it highjacks the mind. To the point where it's difficult to distinguish the mind and our thoughts from fear itself.

So, these tools, like light switches, exist. When fear arises, remember that it is a hallucinated snake or that it's not useful or that it's not real. All three work. There's many more, ones we can come up with ourselves, if we wish. As long as it works, it's valid.

Key is this, when in darkness, have a light switch you've chosen standing by. For example, in writing this book, fear says that I'm risking what people will think of me. Doesn't matter. My role is to recognize it for what it is— hallucinated snake, not useful, not real—and continue on.

I'M IN LOVE

"You're so pretty," I say.

She walks alongside my friend, Gabe, holding his hand. Her dark hair freshly cut, layers. Cool February night in the Mission District in San Francisco. We're heading for tacos.

"I'm in love," she says.

We pause to cross the street.

"It's true," she says, "that's why. I'm in love."

She's pretty regardless, but I get what she's talking about. She glows. Nonstop smile. Full of life.

When I get home, before I go inside, I pause and realize something. The love, it doesn't have to necessarily be for another, does it? Love is an emotion, love is a feeling, love is a way of being. That spring in the step, that smile, that openness, can't it simply come from loving ourselves?

That stops me. Of course. Here we are, thinking that one needs to be in love with another to shine, to feel free and shout from the rooftops, but the most important person, the most important relationship we'll ever have is waiting, is craving to be loved truly and deeply.

And here's the interesting part. When we love ourselves, we naturally shine, we are naturally beautiful. And that draws others to us. Before we know it, they're loving us and it's up to us to choose who to share our love with.

Beautiful irony. Fall in love with yourself. Let your love express itself and the world will beat a path to your door to fall in love with you.

FORGIVENESS

I drive down Highway 1, top down, looking for the trees. Half a mile south of the lighthouse in Pescadero, I see the familiar fence separating the meadow from the road.

I pull over and turn the car off. The engine slowly clicks into silence. Then I grab my daypack, hop the fence, and hike toward the trees. The breeze ripples through the brush as I walk. At the far edge is the open Pacific. Big blue summer sky above.

I discovered this meadow when I first moved to California. I'd get in my car and just drive and drive, amazed by the massive beauty of the Pacific Northwest. There's nothing in the world quite like it.

Years ago, I brought a girlfriend here. When we reached the trees, I tore out a piece of paper from my notebook, handed her a pen.

"You need to forgive yourself," I said to her.

She still carried guilt from her divorce. It was time for her to let it go.

"Write down whatever you're holding against yourself," I said. "Everything. Then forgive yourself. Write that down too. When you're done, we're going to give this paper to the ocean. It'll set you free."

She was quiet for a long while. I think she might have cried a little.

"You have to forgive yourself too," she said. "For not going to medical school."

One amazing thing about women, their wisdom. She was right. I'd chosen start-ups over a career in medicine and no matter what story I told myself, it was a selfish choice. Of money over doing something that mattered to me. A choice I hadn't come to terms with.

So we both worked on our letters, then we hiked down to the waves, balled up the papers, and threw them into the ocean. And you know what, it worked. Something released inside and I never looked back. The regrets about giving up on med school went away. On their own. So simple, this exercise.

Here I am at the grove, once again, this time alone. Only two windswept trees left. The third lies across the grass, the long trunk charred. Lightning strike, perhaps. A shorter trunk sits a few feet apart, bleached white by the wind and rain.

I climb it and stare out at the ocean. Early evening. The sun is high and large. The water below it, all the way to the horizon, shimmers a path of gold.

I pull out my notebook from my daypack, tear off a piece of paper, and write. Today's date. What I'm holding against myself. For screwing up when I knew better. For closing my heart. For hurting more than I needed to. For the mistakes. Everything.

Finished, I write that I forgive myself. For it all. And in that moment of forgiveness, I write that I am clean and pure. Because I know I am.

That is the first step. There are two more left. Life has taught me this much in the time between when I first discovered this grove and today.

I hike down to the beach, sit on a rock, and watch the waves. They crash and crinkle over the pebbly shore. I raise the letter to the sky and read it out loud. All that I hold against myself. All the forgiveness.

I repeat this until it's not needed anymore. Then I reach behind me and grab a large pebble. When I see it, I laugh. It's shaped like a heart. Ah life, you do have a sense of humor.

I fold the paper tight around the stone heart, stare at the waves again. This is a sacred moment. Of giving over all that I held against myself to something bigger. For it to do what it may. For it to take it away from me so that I may unburden myself. So I may live the life I'm meant to live. After all, it's the things we hold against ourselves that weigh us down more than anything.

When the moment feels right, I throw the rock high in an arc into the water. It splashes in a quick plop, then it's gone. The waves rush over and around it. That easy. I watch for a while, wondering if the water will return it to me. It doesn't.

I hike back up to the grove, sit on the trunk again, and pull out the notebook. This time, I write a different letter to myself. Short and to the point:

> *Dear Kamal,*
> *I vow to love you fully and completely and deeply in every way, in all thoughts, in all actions, in all my desires, and my being. I vow to love you, Kamal.*

I sign and date it.

I put the notebook down, stare out at the sun. It's moved halfway down the sky. The wind shimmers through the tall, brown grass. It's getting chilly. I throw on my jacket, take it all in.

Then, back to my notebook, and I read out aloud. My vow to myself. From a clean and pure place. This, my starting point. It feels beautiful. It feels, well . . . it feels right.

That's how you know when you've hit it. When it feels right. No one can teach you this, you just have to do it. And the more you do, the more you develop a trust in this feeling, the more you listen to it, the more you live it. And this transforms your life.

CHOICE

If there's one thing in life I excelled at, it was getting in my own way. If they ever held an Olympics for it, I swear I'd bring home the gold. It was as if as soon as things were going well, I'd find a way to create the biggest obstacle I could find and fall flat on my face.

The pattern served to help keep me unhappy, to definitely not have loving thoughts about myself. Each time, I'd tell myself that I'd learned my lesson. I'd get up, dust myself off, start running, gain speed, life was going good—too good, so of course, the old patterns grew seductive, and, well, splat.

You get the idea . . .

I don't know why I did this. Maybe childhood stuff. Maybe adult stuff. I suppose knowing the reasons help, but in the end, the only thing that matters is the life I live. The results.

Here's one that happened when I started to love myself: I noticed my patterns. I had no idea I even used to do this, I just thought it was my life.

They didn't disappear right away. But I was aware of them. And that was the start. Going forward, each time I got in my way, it was no longer unconscious. It was a choice. And eventually, I grew tired of those choices.

That's the thing about loving yourself, you start to tolerate less what doesn't serve you—especially from yourself. This alone changes your life.

Here's what I've learned about habits and patterns that don't serve us. There is a moment of decision where two paths stretch out in front. One choice calls for the old familiar. The other, unknown. Magic lies in the unknown.

Asking the right question is the most powerful tool I've found in choosing the path to magic. In that moment when I'm about to repeat an old pattern, make a familiar and comfortable mistake, I pause, breathe deep, let the light flow in, and ask myself:

If I loved myself truly and deeply, what would I do?

Sometimes, it helps to expand the question to every level of sappiness I can muster:

If I loved myself truly and deeply, with all my heart, wanting only the very best for myself, wanting and deserving a magical and beautiful life, would I do this?

Then, the choice is mine.

It's such moments that define my life. That define my destiny. And these days, more often than not, I choose a life of love. A life of magic.

GROOVE

A friend lived through some of the fiercest battles American troops endured in the last decade. He and his wife live life full-out. He told me that he lives because the friends he lost would want him to. He lives because he owes it to their memory.

We both lost a mutual friend recently—a former marine who couldn't let go of what he carried from war. Accomplished, humble, hardworking. Yet the ghosts of the past got him.

I've been there—the thought of quitting life a sweet temptation. Just to be done with all this. I've been there closer than I'm comfortable admitting. Fortunately, I've also been on the other side, so that gives me perspective.

I sometimes wonder if thoughts of ending our lives are like an addiction. It's such a primal feeling—to be or not to be—that once you taste the first hit, you're never completely free.

You can leave it behind, yes. But just like an addiction, if you're ever in a bad place and weakened, temptation can rise again.

So what's the solution? Create a new groove that transforms you from the inside out. That creates magic in your life. So if you are ever weakened and old grooves resurface, the new one is so deep and powerful that you see right through the hallucinated snakes.

Simply put, let the light in you remove the darkness. And most importantly, if the old grooves return, reach out for help. To anyone and everyone. One who loves themselves throws aside their ego and asks for help. Because they are worth it.

MAGIC

I finish at the gym, walk outside, and sit on a wall by the driveway. Indian summer evening in San Francisco. Breezy, cool, fog above downtown. Delicious.

I love my life, I find myself thinking, *I love my life, I love my life, I love my life*. The thought flows as naturally as the wind. I watch the skyline—people ask why I let my long hair fall in front of my eyes . . . it's for moments like these, when I watch the world through wisps of silver—*I love my life, I love my life*.

Clouds move above, the thought shifts: *I love myself, I love myself, I love myself, I love myself*. I'm smiling, then grinning. All I am, my hopes, dreams, desires, faults, strengths, everything—*I. Love. Myself*.

If you can reach this point, even if it's for a brief moment, it will transform you—I promise you that.

The key, at least for me, has been to let go. Let go of the ego, let go of attachments, let go of who I think I should be, who others think I should be. And as I do that, the real me emerges, far far better than the Kamal I projected to the world. There is a strength in this vulnerability that cannot be described, only experienced.

Am I this way each moment? No. But I sure as heck am working on it.

Thousands of years ago, a Roman poet wrote, "I am a human being, therefore nothing human is foreign to me." I believe it to be true. So if this is possible for one human, it is possible for anyone. The path might be different, but the destination same.

Key is being open to loving ourselves. Once we do that, life casually takes care of the next steps.

Remain open to that one possibility and you'll experience the beauty of watching the world around you dance its dance, while inside you fully accept this marvelous amazing human being you are. The feeling is, for lack of a better word, magic.

SURRENDER

I once asked a monk how he found peace.

"I say yes," he'd said. "To all that happens, I say yes."

Before I got sick, the last thing my Western mind wanted to say was yes. I was obsessed with my business, with visions of selling it, making enough money to never work again. You can argue that obsession fuels innovation in our society. True, perhaps. But quite often, behind obsession is fear.

And there was plenty of fear. Fear of what people would think. Fear of letting employees and investors down. Fear of failing and what that would mean about me. I used the fear as energy, driving me forward, pushing to achieve, pushing to succeed, paying no attention to my body, to the present, and I paid the price.

Often, the price for not being present is pain.

Now, I understand what the monk meant. There is a surrender to what is, to the moment. Whenever I notice fear in my mind, instead of pushing it aside or using it as fuel, I say to myself, *It's okay*. A gentle yes to myself. To the moment, to what the mind is feeling.

Often, that is enough to deflate the fear. From there, I shift to the truth of loving myself.

Knowing this, I realize that I still could have built a great company, had a beautiful relationship, managed my health, and reached out to my friend before she passed away and told her how much I loved her. I could have done all of this from a place of gentleness, a place of self-love.

But I can't erase the past, only learn from it. It's okay. Applying what I know makes the present and the future a beautiful place to be.

COASTING

As I write this, I'm probably the lowest I've been in a while. Things are just . . . so. Not as bad as they were when I first started, but life's not zinging. The thing is, when life just works for a while, you get used to it and you think it'll stay that way. Recency bias. When things suck, when you're deep in it, it seems like they will suck forever. You can't imagine a way out. When things are great, you live as if it'll always last.

So, I ask myself, *if I was to look deeper, why am I down, why isn't my life an expression of, well, awesomeness?* Once you've experienced it and you know it's possible, then you should be doing everything in your power to keep it that way. It's just too good.

The answer, I'm lazy. When I was sick, I focused on my mind with a desperate intensity. But as life got good, then great, I started to coast. Let the mind drift to its natural devices. Went days, then weeks without meditating. Loving myself became something I assumed, but didn't work toward.

I'm now at the point that when I repeat the loop, "I love myself," it feels strange. I find myself searching for a less powerful word. One that feels right.

But if love isn't right, nothing else will be.

The irony is, I'm the one who shared this truth with friends. "Love yourself," I told them, "see what it did for me. It works, it really works." All true. But who wants to take financial advice from a man barely scraping by?

So I ask myself the question, *If I loved myself, truly and deeply, what would I do?* I love this question. There is no threat, no right or wrong answer, only an invitation to my truth in this present moment.

The answer is simple: I'd commit to the practice. And I would also share the next thing I've learned, which is, don't let yourself coast when things are going great. It's easy to wish for health when you're sick. When you're doing well, you need just as much vigilance.

Honestly, it scares me a little. Coming from the dumps, when life works, it's great. But if life is working, and you do the practice, how high can life go? Can I handle it? Heck, do I even deserve it?

It's a nice trick the monkey mind plays. So I return to the question, *If I loved myself, truly and deeply, what would I do?* The answer comes easy: I'd fly. Fly as high as I possibly can. Then, I'd fly higher.

Now, if you'll excuse me, I'm going to go meditate.

BELIEF

A side effect of loving myself fiercely was that it started
to dislodge old beliefs that I didn't even know existed.
Whether having coffee with a friend or reading a book, I
would have flashes of insight into myself. They were so
clear. It was like my life was a deck of cards, each with a
picture of situations I'd experienced, all falling down at
me, flip flip flip, and the only thought was, *Oh my God, it
all makes sense.*

Here's one example. I've always known that growth
is important to me. If I don't feel like I'm growing, I'm
drifting, depressed. But what I didn't know, until the
practice of self-love showed me, was my belief about
growth: real growth comes through intense, difficult, and
challenging situations.

Can you see how that would define the path of my life?

It was immediately obvious where it came from. The first
time I felt like I grew in a way that I was no longer the
same, I was far better: US Army Infantry boot camp. Was
it intense? Yes. Was it difficult? Yes. Was it challenging?
Every day. Was it happy or joyful? No way. Centuries
of military protocol designed it to be miserable. But it's
something I've always looked at as a defining experience,

one I'm proud of. I went in as an insecure eighteen-year-old. I came out knowing I could handle anything thrown at me. That was growth.

What we believe, that's what we seek, it's the filter we view our lives through. I've actively thrown myself at intense and difficult situations. All situations where I grew, but at what price?

Another example. While building my company, I was known as someone driven to succeed. Many told me so. I thought that as well until I loved myself. Then, one day, I woke up to a spotlight shining on that belief, except the truth was a slight twist: I was driven to not fail.

Huge difference. No wonder my company went the way it did. The intense and consistent work to keep moving it forward, one step away from disaster, always somehow pulling it off, then moving to avert the next disaster. Never failing, but never taking off the way I knew it should.

The good news is that once the spotlight shines from within yourself, there is no going back. The patterns of the mind that held you back fall away on their own. Like rusty old armor you don't need anymore. With each insight, there is freedom, a sense of lightness. And growth.

OXYGEN

After I gave that talk at Renaissance Weekend, one person said to me, "you must love others first."

I respectfully disagree. It's like what they tell you during preflight instructions; in case of emergency, if oxygen masks drop from above, put yours on before you help someone else.

As I started to love myself, things inside me shifted. Fear strengthens the ego. Love softens it. I became more open, vulnerable. It was natural to be gentle with others, even when they weren't loving toward me. And the times it wasn't easy, I had the resources—the loop, the meditation, the mirror, the question—to return to self-love.

There is a power in this. Rather than reacting to situations, I found myself choosing how I wanted to be. That, in turn, created better situations, and ultimately a far better life.

WHERE I WANT TO BE

Lying on my back on a hill, grass slightly tickling my neck.
Beautiful sunny day, blue skies. Clouds drift above. Each,
a thought. I watch, knowing them for what they are.
Rather than attaching my experience of the present to
them, I choose the ones I want to focus on. Or not focus
on. Always my choice.

The thoughts come. Drifting, twisting, turning in shapes.
It is their nature. I pick one for the moment, and then let
it go, never attached. Simply experiencing what I choose.
All through the filter of love. That's it.

END

I think that instead of reading loads of self-help books, attending various seminars, listening to different preachers, we should just pick one thing. Something that feels true for us. Then practice it fiercely.

Place our bet on it, then go all out. That's where magic happens. Where life blows away our expectations.

I found what to bet on. It came from a place of anguish, a place of "no more." But it doesn't have to be that way. It can come from a friend, a book, a lover. It can come from joy.

If something else feels true for you, then do that. I really don't think the details matter. What matters is the practice, the commitment to living your truth.

The results are worth it. I wish that for you.

PART II

THE MANUAL

MY INTENTION

When I wrote Part I, "The Vow," my intention was clear: no matter what objections you had when you started reading, by the time you finished, you would be convinced enough to give loving yourself a shot.

The reason was simple: I'd experienced the magic that loving myself gave me. I'd seen it in others I'd shared the practice with. So I knew that if you just applied what I'd done, you'd experience it too.

And once you experience the magic that results from loving yourself, something inside you is no longer the same. You may coast, you may quit, but you can never lie to yourself about what is possible.

Part II, "The Manual," is the result of responding to thousands of readers' emails. I learned from them that even though Part I succeeded, it wasn't enough. There were two key questions I still had to cover.

The first, *How can I apply this to my life easily?* The second, *How do I make it last?*

My intention is to resolve these threads. As a result, I want to give you a definitive manual for loving yourself. One that is easy, effective, and lasts.

So here is a step-by-step guide to loving yourself. It takes the original practice and goes deeper. Then it adds what I've learned over the years to make it more impactful. By the time you finish, you'll understand that loving yourself is not only possible, but stupidly simple.

Most importantly, you will know exactly how to do it.

JUMP

I don't know what brought you to this book or where you are in your life. But this I know: we can always be better; we can always start anew. There is no perfect time for it. No preparation or particular state of mind required. There is only commitment in this moment.

It's like standing at the edge of a cliff over the ocean. You can take as many deep breaths as you want, but in the end, you gotta jump.

Here's how we're going to do it:

First, we will dig the foundation. You will forgive yourself and make your vow. These acts are a declaration to life itself. They change everything.

Then, you will dive into the practice—mental loop, meditation, mirror, question—and learn the nuances of each. You will learn how to apply the practice to your life and how to make it last. This will cement the foundation.

Finally, we will build on the foundation. How loving yourself applies to your past, present, and future; how to use this to give love to another; what to do if you're ever suffering; and how to use your love to connect to something bigger than you. We will wrap up with practical advice on how to live this way of life.

I will guide you and where it's helpful, I'll break down exactly what to do. Everything will be from my experience. And since we're both human, what worked for me will work for you.

I have one suggestion: don't get entangled in the details. If ever confused, remember that it's your intention that matters. And the only intention you need here is pure and focused love for yourself.

Ready? Let's jump . . .

FIRST, FORGIVE YOURSELF

Before you step into the future, you must release the shackles of the past.

I don't understand why we work so hard to forgive others without forgiving the only one we have any power over— ourselves. All freedom starts within. Even if you want to forgive others, you must forgive yourself first. Only the free can free another.

It took me a while to understand this. But once I applied it, this added a level to loving myself I hadn't experienced before. It's easy and absolutely liberating.

Imagine letting go of what you've held against yourself. That's what this does. And it leads you perfectly to the vow to love yourself.

TRY THIS:
FORGIVE YOURSELF

Step 1: Go somewhere where you won't be interrupted. The less distraction for anything you apply in this manual, the better. My favorite place for this is in nature. At the very least, choose someplace that makes you feel good.

Step 2: When you are ready, write down all that you hold against yourself. Every single thing. Please don't hold anything back. This is your healing. It is sacred. Whatever emotions rise, feel fully and let them pass. You are worth the magic you will experience afterward.

Step 3: Once the emotions have passed, remember that you are a human being. Therefore, it's your nature to make mistakes. It's the contract of existing on this planet. Sit with that for a moment.

Step 4: Write down that you forgive yourself. Read the whole thing out loud. Again and again and again until you feel something inside shift.

You might need to write it down multiple times to feel the shift. If so, then write it, read it out loud, and repeat until you're ready to let go. Remember, you are worth this.

Step 5: Take the paper you wrote on and destroy it.

You can tear it up. You can throw it in the ocean or lake or river. You can chuck it in the garbage or set it on fire or flush it down the toilet. You can put it on a rocket and launch it into outer space.

It really doesn't matter how you destroy it. You're throwing away everything you held against yourself. The act itself is symbolic. It's the purity of intention that matters.

Let this action take the paper—and all that it represents—away from you. Let life take it from you. Let love take it from you. Let it go. You are forgiven by the one person you need it from most—yourself.

SECOND, YOUR VOW

When I first wrote the vow to love myself, I was desperate. I had to save myself. I remember how tightly I gripped that pen, how it dug through the paper and onto the wooden desk.

When I finished, I put the pen down and stared at my journal. What had I done?

In front of me, in my handwriting in black ink, was a vow. And a vow is a full-on commitment. A sacred act to oneself. There was no escape from this.

I didn't know how to love myself, but because of the vow, I had to figure it out. So, hiding in my bedroom, day after day and night after night, I worked on myself until I did.

This took a man who was deep in failure and hating himself to a man who was loving himself, loving life, and experiencing magic in ways he never knew existed. And years later, still does. Even more so.

That is the power of a vow. It changes everything.

You go all in. There is no turning back. No trying or wanting or wishing. You're doing. If you stumble and fall, you get up, dust yourself off, and continue on. And there is only one way—forward.

Looking back, I'm still amazed that I actually figured out how to love myself. But it doesn't surprise me anymore. I've learned that when you make a true commitment to yourself, things start to shift. Inside and outside. You can feel life ripple around you.

And please trust me on this—just because I was at bottom doesn't meant that you must be. Every single moment in our lives is an opportunity to commit. No matter where we are, no matter how good or bad things may seem, this moment is the perfect moment to take our stand. To say *no more* to what doesn't serve us and an all-in *yes* to what does.

It really is this simple. I swear to you.

I've used commitments to transform my health, my fitness, my finances, my relationships. And, of course, the commitment that changed everything—to love myself. I make it again and again.

Life is more expansive than our human minds can comprehend. Who we are spreads out in ways bigger than us. So when we make ourselves better, those around us are better for it. Then, those around them. And so on.

The results of our commitments are far greater than the original impact.

For example, the vow to love myself transformed my life. But it didn't stop there. When I shared the practice with friends, it made their lives better. In turn, they convinced me to write it down. Because of that one vow, here you are, reading my truth.

We have no way to foresee the magic that results from our commitments. This is bigger than us. We just have to trust in it. And it will happen each and every time.

Here's a side effect of making and keeping commitments to yourself: your self-confidence skyrockets. You walk through life differently. That's the best way I can describe it.

Things you once feared become attainable because you know that all it takes is a commitment to yourself, going all in, and through the process, you'll figure out the path and go further than you thought possible. You naturally develop a healthy respect for the person you've become.

If you think about it, this is a fantastic way to love yourself.

TRY THIS:
MAKE YOUR VOW

Do this immediately after forgiving yourself. You've just left the past behind. There is no better time to step into your future.

Step 1: Sit somewhere quiet with a piece of paper and pen. There's something powerful about writing a vow with your hand, seeing the words flow through the pen, feeling the page. I've tried this on a computer and phone but haven't experienced the same power.

Step 2: Write the vow to love yourself truly and deeply in every way you can. Make it so powerful that it scares you a little. If you want, use mine as a guide.

It can be as long or short as you want. The key is, it has to inspire something inside you.

Step 3: If you feel the need to edit your vow, rewrite the whole thing again. Feel the power of the complete vow. The more energy you put into this, the more you'll receive.

Step 4: Read the vow out loud. Again and again until you feel it vibrate inside you.

Step 5: Put this paper somewhere you'll see it daily, preferably multiple times a day. For me, it's a journal on my desk. But really, it doesn't matter where. You know the right place for you.

You can also carry a photo of it as a reminder. But if your life allows it, return to that place with the vow daily. After a while, you'll notice your mind naturally fall into the power of the vow—and the results—whenever you return to that paper. It is a physical record of your commitment to yourself. Your subconscious will recognize it.

Step 6: Read it daily. At the very minimum, twice—once in the beginning of the day, once at the end. The more often you do this, the deeper the groove.

You can read it out loud or in your head. But each time, make yourself feel the power of your vow. Imagine how you would be if you truly and unconditionally loved yourself. Imagine how your life would be. Feel that. This imagining and feeling part is important. Don't skip it.

If you do this again in the future—and I hope you do—write a new vow from scratch. Your vow should reflect who you are at this moment in your life. It will have greater impact this way.

TEN BREATHS

Before we dive into the practice itself, I want to share one thing that's made it sustainable. You might laugh at the simplicity of it. And that simplicity is exactly why it works.

Throughout the day, I pause whatever I'm doing, and take ten breaths. That's it.

But these aren't your average breaths. They are deep and slow and purposeful. A complete shift from my thoughts to a pure focus on loving myself.

When I breathe in, I say to myself, *I love myself*. I feel light enter from above, doing what it does. When I breathe out, I let the light remove whatever needs to go. No control, no forcing, just allowing. A surrender of sorts.

I originally came up with this to overcome my laziness. No matter how good things got, eventually, I'd start coasting. I needed to create a process that would be so easy, there was no way I couldn't do it. And that's what this has done.

Remember, if you want full-on magic, go all in. Focus every single conscious breath on loving yourself. So this doesn't bypass that. What it does do is keep the momentum going if you get lazy. And it's so efficient that you have no excuse to skip it.

If you ever see me in the gym, you'll notice me walk to the mirror after a workout and stare into my eyes for a few moments, then grin. You just caught me doing the ten breaths mirror.

Or, outside my building, you'll see me pause, look up at the sky for a while, and then go in. I just did the ten breaths mental loop.

My day is filled with these moments. And why not? They feel good, they deepen the groove of loving myself, and they create magic in my life. Most importantly, I can do them anywhere and anytime.

As we go through the practice in the rest of this manual, we'll weave in the ten breaths so you can see how I do it. That should give you ideas on how to add it to your life.

THIRD, DO THE PRACTICE

My first career was in clinical research. I was fresh out of college, gathering data in hospital emergency departments, hoping the experience would help me get into medical school.

As life has it, I fell in love with writing. Then, I discovered start-ups, and medical school never happened. But the experience left its mark. In some ways, it led to the practice.

After I made the vow, I had no idea how to love myself. Who among us ever got that training? So I started trying anything and everything in my head. I tried every stupid thing I could dream of. I didn't care if it seemed foolish or too simple. I only cared about one thing: that it worked.

Basically, I was running clinical trials in my head. Sample size of the one person I had to save—myself.

Here's how I knew if something worked: it shifted me away from the misery I was in. If it did, I would do it more, go deeper. If it stopped working or grew weaker, I threw it away. I had no attachment to anything except results.

Ultimately, four things were left:

- The mental loop
- The meditation
- The mirror
- The question

If I was to give you a timeline, the mental loop came first.
Then, the meditation. Then, the mirror. The question
came when I was dealing with people and their dramas.
Each worked in its own way.

You might be tempted to only do one. Don't fall for that
trap. Although each is powerful, put them together, and
their effects compound. That's what created magic in my
life.

Besides, you just made a vow to love yourself. You owe it
to yourself to go all in.

THE PRACTICE:
I. MENTAL LOOP

After I wrote the vow and was trying out anything that might work, I noticed that while repeating, "I love myself," there were brief moments where I made myself actually believe it.

At first, it felt like I'd tricked my mind. It was normal to hate myself, to be miserable, so this burst of feeling love for myself, even if it was for a second or two, it felt, well . . . it felt strange.

But there was something there. Something special. Deep down, I knew.

The more I felt the feeling, the faster my state of mind shifted. So I consciously added feeling to the mental loop. I actually made myself feel love for myself. This was the nuance that took me to the next level.

The more I did this, the better I got. The better life got. It's as if thoughts and feelings added together create transformation on a higher level than thoughts alone.

After a while, this grew easier. The groove was growing deeper. I still remember when I first felt the feeling rise on its own. I was outside my building, staring up at the sky, and it hit me so strong—this feeling of loving myself. So natural. So real.

I had to capture the moment. Perhaps to remind myself that it'd actually happened. I still didn't believe this was my reality and was afraid that it would disappear. I ran upstairs to my apartment and wrote the chapter titled, "Magic."

When you do the mental loop with feeling, it will feel strange at first. You might feel like you're faking it. That it's not real. In that case, ask yourself this: *Is the noise in my head real?*

It's just loops upon thought loops, old grooves and patterns running themselves. Confetti of the mind. Let's say you resolve something in your head, a new version will pop up tomorrow. Even if you let go of anger against someone today, you might feel anger against a different person next week. Nothing's changed except window dressing.

That's why this one groove is so effective. Since we're already wired for love, it pierces through the clutter, shakes the garbage out naturally. Old thought patterns lose their power.

When I was at bottom, I didn't care why my mind favored fear-based thoughts. If you're on fire, you don't want a lecture on the nature of combustion. You want water. So, rather than fighting the thoughts in my head, I focused on the only one that mattered. The one that saved me. I was, as a wise friend said, living life from the inside out.

That is what got me here. That is what the mental loop is all about.

TRY THIS:
MENTAL LOOP

The mental loop is the simplest piece of the practice. Just repeat "I love myself" every chance you get. Either out loud or in your head, whatever feels right. That's it.

What you're doing is shifting the mind to one focused groove. You're pulling out the rag, cleaning your window. Light will enter. It always does.

Your mind might rebel. After all, it's not normal to consciously narrow our thoughts down to just one. It's a form of mental discipline we've never been taught. So, memories and emotions will probably rise, telling you the opposite.

First, this is to be expected. Be gentle with yourself and continue. The very act of creating this new groove is a form of loving yourself.

Second, don't listen to the fears. Hallucinated snakes, every single one. To save yourself, you must step through them.

When a hero sets off on a quest, he knows that there will be obstacles along his path to treasure. That's part of the grand adventure. You are the hero of your story. Hallucinated snakes are your obstacles.

Third, stepping through hallucinated snakes builds trust in yourself. You realize that you are more powerful than your illusions. But no book or person can do this for you. Only you can.

Once you're slightly used to the mental loop—and it only takes a day or two—add feeling. It will take you to the next level.

Why even wait? Because the mind rebels harder if you do it all in the beginning. So the best way to do it is step by step. Start the groove, then dig deeper. Water will flow.

To add feeling, breathe slow and purposeful breaths. With the in-breath, say "I love myself," and feel love rise within your chest. It helps to picture it as light. With the out-breath, release whatever comes. There is no forcing or faking. It's more of an allowing because your love is already inside you.

The more you do this, the deeper the groove. The more it becomes part of your subconscious. The more it starts to run on its own, until eventually, your mind is more an expression of this groove than it's not.

Some prefer saying, "I love me." Others, "I am loved." All variations work. Remember, it's the intention behind the words that matters. In this case, your intention must be a pure focus on love for yourself.

When you first start, be obsessive about the mental loop. Do it as much as you possibly can. You'll notice the inner shifts, then the outer. Go all in.

But eventually, if you're like me and things start to get really good, you'll slow down. That's fine. Life is long and has its own rhythm. But here's the danger: if you stop, the mind starts to slide to old ways.

It never goes back to where you once were—you've created a powerful new groove, after all—but the grooves of the past run deep. They've been dug in over a lifetime. That's what you're up against.

Here is how to keep it consistent:

WHEN YOU WAKE UP

Take a long and deep breath and say in your mind or aloud, "I love myself." Imagine light flowing in from above into your head and spreading to your body, going wherever it needs to go. Feel the feeling of loving yourself. Then, exhale.

Do this for ten breaths. It's a beautiful way to start the day.

DURING THE DAY

Whenever you notice your thoughts wander to darkness—anger, hurt, pain, fear, and so on—pull out your rag, wipe your window.

Let *shift* be your action. If you notice your mind in a negative loop, shift to love for yourself. Do this throughout the day. Shift. Shift. Shift.

Each time you shift, do the mental loop intensely for ten deep breaths. If you're ever having a hard moment or feel stressed, pausing to do this really helps. It will also show you that ultimately, we're responsible for our misery as well as our healing. And healing is available to us in each and every moment.

Remember, you're deepening this new groove with each shift. What might feel like work in the beginning will eventually become natural. The groove will run on its own.

FALLING ASLEEP

Just repeat what you did when you woke. Except here, don't stop. Do it until you fall asleep.

Your mind will wander, as it naturally does, but each time you notice, shift it back to your new groove. This is an incredibly effective time. You're layering love for yourself into your subconsciousness as you drift into sleep.

It's also a beautiful way to end the day.

THE PRACTICE:
2. MEDITATION

The meditation is the most powerful part of the practice.

But you might not feel the effects immediately. Often, you're just sitting there with your mind wandering all over the place, wondering what you're doing with your life, how you ended up here, why your nose itches, if you can get a refund on this book . . .

Yet, even with all this, there are moments of silence. Of your mind getting out of the way. Of light entering. And those moments are enough.

Remember, it's the light that heals. It's the light that transforms. There is nothing for us to do but to let it in. No forcing, just allowing.

What really helped me was doing this to the same piece of music. It was something I had positive associations with. Since I felt good listening to it, it was easier to go into that state when I closed my eyes to meditate. Within a week, the moment the song came on, my mind automatically went into a silent state. Light poured in.

I can't promise how you'll feel when you start this. But I can promise that if you do it and focus on the light coming in from above, allowing it in, soon enough, you will notice shifts within yourself. And this I promise you as well—in your life.

TRY THIS: MEDITATE

The meditation is simple. Find a piece of music that makes you feel good, play it, close your eyes, feel light enter from above with each in-breath, and say to yourself, *I love myself*.

Then, release whatever comes with the out-breath. If your mind wanders, gently return it to your in-breath. Do this until the music ends. For me, this takes slightly over seven minutes.

Your mind might rebel, but don't let this scare you. Remember, there are hallucinated snakes along the path to love. Once you recognize them for the illusions that they are, their power over you naturally lessens. That, in itself, is worth it.

Repeat the meditation daily to the same music. If you can, at the same time each day. Make it an anchor that your life spins around. After the first few times, add feeling exactly as you did with the mental loop.

I don't recommend listening to that music outside of the meditation. You don't want the mind to connect it to the mundane. This is a focused and beautiful time when you're pulling out the rag, cleaning the window, letting light enter. Keep it special.

THE PRACTICE:
3. MIRROR

This is the one that many avoid. Here's my suggestion:
if you find yourself resisting, then you must do it. The
resistance is old loops and patterns fighting for survival.
The same ones that have held you down. Time to let
them go.

I stumbled upon this by accident. One night, while doing
the mental loop out loud, I stared at myself in the mirror.
And I continued . . . "I love myself. I love myself. I love
myself. . . ."

Whoa. Something powerful was happening.

I was connecting to myself in a deeper way. After just five
minutes, I felt a buzzing. Yet it felt like things had settled
inside. Like they were more solid. It was the strangest
thing.

I continued this daily. The trick, I learned by trying out
every variation, was to look into my eyes. Not my face.
Not my hair. Not anywhere else. But to put myself so
close to the mirror that I could only see my eyes, then tell
myself that I loved myself.

This anchors our love to our physical selves. And the focus on the eyes avoids the judgments we make about our faces and bodies. The more we do this, the more the judgments disappear.

This one is special. It makes you fall in love with yourself.

TRY THIS:
MIRROR

Stare into your eyes in the mirror and do the mental loop nonstop for five minutes. When you can, pause between breaths and get lost in your eyes. The more you do this, the more you'll experience your own beauty.

Then, just like the mental loop and meditation, add feeling after the first few times.

I don't recommend doing anything else, like brushing your teeth, while doing this. As for the best time, do it right after the meditation if you can. Done back to back in the morning, they set up your day.

I've found it to be more powerful when saying "I love myself" out loud. If that's too much, then whisper. Something happens when you combine the physicality of your voice repeating that it loves you with staring into your own eyes. It causes an internal shift, lets the light in.

The key here is focus. You're going all in on loving yourself for these brief five minutes. In a visceral and physical way. Give yourself this gift.

THE PRACTICE:
4. QUESTION

It's easy to get caught in our heads, run thought loops on automatic. This feels so normal that we rarely stop to question it. Yet most of these loops don't serve us. At worst, they destroy our self-worth, separate us from love.

That's why the right question in the moment is effective. First, it shifts the mind. We're no longer on automatic pilot. Second, answering forces us to make a conscious choice. Third, choice leads to action, internal and external.

Asking and answering questions make us proactive in our lives, rather than reactive. This, in itself, is transformative. Here are the ones I use for loving myself:

If I loved myself truly and deeply,
would I let myself experience this?

The *if* removes any arguments the mind creates. Even when I'm feeling horrible in the moment and not loving myself, the *if* makes the answer possible and real.

This question is perfect for dealing with others. No matter how someone else may be, how I feel inside is my choice. Always. So I ask the question to shift away from reactive thoughts.

If I loved myself truly and deeply,
what would I do?

This question is great for life choices. It focuses me forward, rather than on the rearview mirror of my thoughts. No matter what's happened, no matter the mistakes I've made, it leads me to what I need. In fact, you're reading this book because of this question.

After I'd finished the original version and committed to publishing it, I still hesitated. I was terrified about ruining my career in Silicon Valley. Then, one evening, I asked myself the question.

The answer was simple: I'd share my truth. It was too important not to. If I was mocked, then I'd love myself through it. Magic would result either way—what it would be, I had no idea. But I'd experienced enough magic from loving myself to *know* it as real.

Answering this question shifted my thoughts from fear to truth, and then to action. It put the book out to the world. So much magic has come into my life as a result.

If you ever feel helpless or lost, ask yourself this. It will guide you to choice and action.

Am I in light or darkness?

When I notice myself lost in thought, I ask myself this question.

If the answer is "light," great. I ramp up the thoughts and enjoy them. By the way, the more you love yourself, the more you find yourself here.

If it's fear, anger, righteous stories, hurt, it's all darkness. There is no way to fight it or push it away. That only makes it stronger. That only pulls me away from the present moment.

So I return to what I know works. I pull out my rag, wipe my window—I go to the ten breaths of loving myself. Sometimes, this shifts me from darkness right away. Sometimes, it takes many more breaths, all depending on how entangled I was in my thoughts. But it works.

TRY THIS: QUESTION

You might be tempted to use all three, but I'll caution against it. If you're not used to asking and answering questions in the moment, multiple options will cause the mind to hesitate. That's often enough time for old loops to slip through.

A question is another light switch. You just have to get in the habit of flipping it. Once you've deepened the groove and it becomes natural, then add the others.

Start with this: *If I loved myself truly and deeply, what would I do?*

It's easy to remember and applies to pretty much any thought or situation. Just this alone will improve the quality of your life.

Here's how to deepen the groove:

Pick one thing that's important to you. It could be a relationship, it could be your health, a personal or business goal. Then, ask yourself the question every time you're involved in the activity.

For example, if it's health, whenever you're about to eat, ask yourself, "If I loved myself truly and deeply, what would I do?"

The answer will shift you away from old patterns to choice, then action. Once it starts to feel natural, use it for other areas of your life.

I've used this question in writing this manual. My commitment is to give it everything I've got. So, whenever I get tempting requests that pull me away from writing, I ask myself, "If I loved myself truly and deeply, what would I do?" Then, I live the answer.

Questions, more than anything, will steer you away from what doesn't serve you, both in your mind and in your life.

THE NEXT LEVEL

We first started the groove by saying, "I love myself" with the in-breath and releasing whatever rose with the out-breath. Then, we dug deeper and added feeling. This shifted us away from darkness to light.

There's another level. You'll be ready for it once you notice your out-breath change. It will feel cleaner, more peaceful. It's time to dig deeper, again.

With the out-breath, say, "thank you." With feeling.

After all, if you're loving yourself and experiencing magic, gratitude is a natural response. Who or what the gratitude is for is up to you. What matters is the feeling of gratitude itself.

Once again, it's simple to do. Say "I love myself," with the in-breath, say "thank you" with the out-breath," and feel the emotion of each. Do this for the mental loop, meditation, and mirror.

When you breathe in light and breathe out gratitude, it leaves no space for darkness. Do this enough and eventually, this loop starts to run on its own. That's where you want to be: where love and gratitude are natural expressions of each breath. It's beautiful to experience.

You might be tempted to start here and you're welcome to try. It's your life and the only results that matter are yours. But here's what I've learned: if you jump in hard, the mind rebels equally harder. Those hallucinated snakes fight dirty. But if you go step by step, there is less resistance. The process is gentler and you're more likely to succeed.

I got here by starting the groove, observing what rose inside, then deepening it in whatever way felt natural. No map needed. Just like every other human, I was already wired for love. Once I accepted this, the groove practically dug itself.

RITUALS

In basic training, before we entered our barracks, we had to do twenty push-ups. It didn't matter if you were exhausted or had to go in and out all day. Before you went inside, you did your push-ups.

We had a whole series of these. From the range to the cafeteria, there were always push-ups and pull-ups to be done. These alone probably got more than a few recruits in shape. Months after, anytime I entered a building, I still had to suppress the urge to drop down and give twenty. That ritual had been hardwired into me.

I took this concept and applied it to the practice. This took what I knew I should do and put it on autopilot.

For example, whenever I sit down to write, I close my eyes, breathe deep, and feel love for myself. I feel gratitude for the words that are to come. And, since this mental loop grows stronger each time, it shifts me to loving myself, and the words flow.

Meditating in the morning, ten breaths before entering my building, ten breaths at waking and before sleep—all rituals I've created for myself.

You don't waste minutes each morning wondering whether you should brush your teeth or not. You just do it. That's the power of rituals. They create the grooves we call habits. And these habits, both good and bad, run our lives.

Create Love Yourself rituals for your morning, your bedtime, and whatever you repeat during the day. Anything from eating to business meetings. The more you add the practice to your natural rhythm, the more it becomes a part of you.

Please don't skip this. Rituals are a practical application of your vow. Without them, you will most likely find yourself putting off what you need. Without rituals, we risk letting what should come first come last.

In fact, if you're ever going through a rough patch, dial up your rituals. Meditate more than once. Do the mirror every chance you can get. Make your day a constant practice of the ten breaths. This will help pull you out.

TRACK

An object at rest stays at rest unless acted upon by a force. This is Newton's first law of motion, sometimes called the law of inertia. A rocket on a pad will stay there forever unless the boosters are ignited. Same in our loving ourselves. The vow is the energy needed for liftoff.

But how do you keep the rocket going?

In our case, how do you continue loving yourself once the initial excitement has worn off? How do you do the practice when responsibilities get in the way or you just don't feel like it? Simple. You track yourself.

Get a calendar, and at the end of each day, check off the various parts of the practice you've done. If you hit your full commitment, put a big X through that day. There is a deep sense of satisfaction at seeing an unbroken string of X's.

Our minds are experts at crafting stories on why slipping is justified. These are old mental loops fighting for survival. That's why being accountable outside ourselves works. No matter the excuse, empty squares on a calendar don't lie. They make us face the truth on where we're falling short.

I didn't do this when I first started. But later, as life started to work and I got lazy and coasted, I found that the act of tracking naturally made me step up. It was that easy.

Besides, it's better to correct yourself before life does. By the time life intervenes to get your attention, the wake-up call is usually painful.

LINE IN THE SAND

No matter how intense the vow, no matter the tracking, odds are that along the way, we will slip. We'll miss parts of the practice. We'll get lazy and coast. It's important to be honest with ourselves about this. And plan for it.

First, don't beat yourself up. I have yet to see a photo of a human being under the headline "Perfect." To fall and get up is part of the contract of being alive.

Second, pick something in the practice that you will not skip, no matter what. This is your line in the sand. It is the bare minimum you will do to keep your vow.

The meditation is my line in the sand. No matter how the day unfolds, I won't go to sleep without doing it. This way, even if I fail at keeping my full commitment to myself, at least I kept the most important part to me. And that allows the momentum to continue. Then, the next day, I return to the full practice.

These lines in the sand keep momentum going:

- Meditation once a day.
- Mirror once a day.
- Ten breaths of the mental loop ten times a day.

Pick one that feels most powerful, then do it. But remember, return to the full practice as soon as you can. That's where magic happens fastest.

IN A NUTSHELL

There you have it: forgive yourself, make your vow, and do the practice. All from the inside out.

There is no perfection here. No forcing or trying to make anything happen. Only commitment and allowing. Letting light enter, doing what it does. We are all capable of this. No matter what we've experienced in our lives, we're all hardwired for love.

I've come to believe that living this way taps us into the flow of life. Rather than fight or struggle, we go with the natural evolution of things. Perhaps that's why not only our inside shifts, our outside does as well.

After you forgive yourself and make your vow, do the practice for a month straight. That's what it initially took for my life to transform. This works for readers I've spoken with as well.

When we attach our commitments to time, they suddenly become real. And as a result, far more likely to happen. So hold yourself accountable to your vow for one month. Track yourself, pick your line in the sand, and create your rituals. Go all in. It's only one month to love yourself truly and deeply and transform your life.

The rest of this manual includes what I've added to loving myself over the years. Use what feels right, but keep the practice as your foundation.

CHILDHOOD STRINGS

I've always had a difficult time with breakups. It's as if at the end of each relationship, I forget my own value and devolve. It's a deeply entrenched groove, which is why an alternative groove through a consistent practice is a must. Otherwise, the mind returns to the suffering it knows.

While doing the meditation, I realized why I had this groove. My father was abusive to my mother. After one especially bad episode, she went grocery shopping and didn't return. We'd planned this out, she and I. When my father went to sleep, I'd sneak out with my little brother and meet her around the corner.

My father caught me. I still remember that moment. Looking down those stairs, that locked door so far away. I tried escaping multiple times, no luck.

Then one afternoon, my father took us to meet her at the park. We sat on a bench while he convinced her to return. But he wouldn't let me touch her. I will never forget that feeling, that ache of wanting so badly to reach out, to have her hold me.

Any surprise I lose it after the end of a relationship? In those moments, it's not this grown adult who has his act together and knows how life works. It's that little boy, pulling the strings, desperately needing love.

But no one else can fill that for him. No relationship, no object, no substance or escape. Only I can. So the last time this happened, I turned inward, closed my eyes, and pictured him. Then, I held him and loved him. Just loved him.

And you know what, that's all he needed. He calmed down. Whenever he tugs again, I do the same. It's another opportunity to love a piece of me.

We all have our weaknesses. This happens to be one of mine. Yours might be different, but the themes are the same. We're human and the primal threads of love and fear bind us all.

Whatever childhood strings you discover within yourself, first, accept them. They are a part of your personal history. They've made you this amazing beautiful human being that you are.

Second, love that part of yourself. In the present, give yourself what you needed in the past, and you will understand the truth—you are what you needed all along.

TRY THIS:
CHILDHOOD STRINGS

Step 1: Sit or lie down somewhere quiet. As always, if you can, choose a place that makes you feel good.

Step 2: Close your eyes and do the mental loop. Breathe in love, breathe out whatever comes. Let light flow in from above. Do this until you feel a natural rhythm.

Step 3: Place your hand over your heart. This same heart once beat for your younger self.

Step 4: When you are ready, picture the child in front. If emotions rise from either of you, be patient and let them flow.

Step 5: Feel your heartbeat for a little while. It belongs to you both. You are in sync.

Step 6: Then, give the child your love.

You can hold the child and say, "I love you, I love you, I love you . . ." You can stand apart and do it.

You can feel light flow through you and into the child, dissolving all that needs to go. You can be silent or you can speak your love out loud.

The details don't matter. The only thing that matters is your intention: to give this child love. To give it all the love you've got.

Step 7: Don't be surprised if long-suppressed emotions rise. Release them and be free.

Step 8: There is nothing to solve, nothing to fix, nothing else to do. Once you've given your love and feel calm, open your eyes.

Step 9: Feel your heartbeat again for a little while. Then, you're done.

Here's a suggestion: Why limit this to your childhood self? There's nothing stopping you from giving love to who you were last year or even yesterday. This is especially helpful if you've recently gone through something difficult.

Give your past self the love you needed. It's one of the most powerful things you can do.

YOUR FUTURE SELF

One day, after giving my younger self love, I asked myself, *Someday, I'll be older and wiser. What would that man say to me today?*

The question made me sit up, excited. My future self who's been through everything I have and beyond. Who has the benefit of hindsight that I don't. Who has love and compassion for me in a way that only one who's walked in my shoes can. Who understands me better than anyone ever could.

The answer was obvious. He would do exactly what I just did for my younger self.

So I closed my eyes, did the mental loop, and imagined him standing in front. He smiled a loving and understanding smile. And then, he hugged me, kissed the top of my head, and gave me love.

There was nothing for me to do. Only receive love. My love.

Do this.

GIVING LOVE

If I'm ever having issues with someone I care for deeply, I do the mental loop, imagine myself holding this person close, and then I kiss the top of their head and give them love. That's it.

This shifts me from anger, hurt, or resentment. Darkness, all. Light flows through, healing whatever I hold between us. It reminds me of what matters.

When you do this, remember one thing: the point is to shift yourself, not the other person. And don't ever fear that by giving love, you will have less for yourself.

Love is not a beggar's bowl. Love is a deep well connected to life itself. The more it flows through you, the more it transforms you, and the more you receive in return.

PARACHUTE

Sometimes, loving ourselves can be the hardest thing to do. Especially if we're caught up in suffering. If you find yourself there, tell yourself this: *Life loves me.*

If you believe in God, then replace "Life" with "God." Or just make "Life" that single spark that resulted in billions of galaxies and, ultimately, you. This connects you to something bigger than you.

Tell yourself this again and again and again. In fact, set everything aside and meditate, using this as the loop. As you breathe in, receive the light. Imagine what you're saying to be true, be in the place of how that feels. This is important. Don't just say it intellectually, experience it.

Release everything that comes with the out-breath. Repeat this until the only thing that arises when you breathe out is a simple "thank you."

When you're finished with the meditation, return to that place in your head every chance you get. Even if it's for ten breaths. Do it until it's your dominant thought.

This is a parachute. It will help you. Even if you don't believe it for a single second, it will help you. Parachutes work regardless of your beliefs on gravity and air resistance.

First, it will distance you from the disempowering stories of the mind. Second, it will take you outside yourself and to the statistically remarkable gift of just being alive. Third, it will remind you of your own worthiness to be loved.

Once you have shifted, return to loving yourself. But use this anytime you need.

HIGHER

I believe that we are part of something bigger than us. Like sparks of a greater fire. Loving myself showed me that. Too much outside my scope of control shifted in my life for me to rationalize it away.

You don't need to believe what I do. Life works the way it does, regardless. But I want to share how I've used this to take the practice to a higher level.

In the last chapter, I gave you a parachute. I use the same principle here. But rather than waiting until I need it, I mix it in with loving myself. Here's what I do:

I close my eyes, feel light envelop me from above, and with each in-breath, I say, "I love myself" a few times. Then, I shift to Bigger Than Me loving me. You can call it Life or God or the Universe or whatever sits right with you.

I shift the phrases back and forth on instinct. Most importantly, I let myself feel what it would be like if I loved myself plus I was loved by all that is. It's absolutely beautiful to experience.

With the out-breath, I release whatever comes. But I make sure that by the time I'm done, the out-breath gives a natural "thank you." That's it.

You can do this with the mental loop, meditation, and mirror. Your groove will deepen.

REPEAT

Let's imagine that you've forgiven yourself. You've made the vow. You've gone all in. You live, breathe, and eat the practice daily. You realize that you won't do it perfectly each day. What matters is your intention and consistency over time.

Perhaps you beat yourself up when you slipped here and there. But you've let that go. After all, beating yourself up isn't the most loving thing to do.

You have shifted on the inside. Your life has shifted on the outside. You are zinging. The month is up. I have a question for you . . .

If you loved yourself truly and deeply,
what would you do?

My suggestion: don't stop. Please.

The grooves of the past are strong. Don't let them regain a foothold in your consciousness. Recommit. Deepen the groove of loving yourself. The more you do this, the more it'll become a part of your being. Of who you are.

Do the whole process again—forgive yourself, make your vow, and do the practice.

If this sounds like work, it isn't. A month will have shown you magic. Accept that as your new normal and build from there. One more month of loving yourself. A higher normal. And then another month . . .

Imagine a year of this. You will not recognize your life. I promise you that.

IF IT SCARES YOU

One of the most transformative lessons of loving myself has been this:

If it scares me, there is magic on the other side.

I cannot emphasize this enough. If there's ever a rule for life, this is it.

Look, any of us could fill a book with our fears and all the perfectly legitimate and beautifully crafted reasons for them. But they don't serve us. Only stepping through fear does.

Here is what loving myself gave me: I recognized fear for what it was—hallucinated snake, not useful, not real. Then, I loved myself and stepped through. Each time, magic.

Even if life didn't give me the exact result I was hoping for, stepping through fear led me down paths that were equally rewarding, if not better. Usually better.

This practice of stepping through fear again and again taught me that fear is not something to always be avoided. It's a signal, just like any other. Perfect for avoiding burning infernos or thousand-foot plummets. But outside of that, it's a sign toward where magic is.

And life requires me to step through. I don't know why, but that's just the way it is.

Try this for yourself. Step through your hallucinated snakes. It's a practical application of loving yourself. Each day, pick one and step through. Sometimes you'll have to step through the same fear a gazillion times. Doesn't matter. You're deepening the groove. You're becoming a person who steps through fear.

Step through until it's more of who you are than who you're not. Until it's a natural habit. And don't forget to enjoy the magic on the other side. You've earned it.

EXPECT MAGIC

When I first started the practice, I got better on the inside. Then, life got better on the outside. I started to experience synchronicities that I couldn't explain. The most honest way to state it is this: life just started to work.

The more I loved myself, the more life worked out for me in ways I couldn't have planned. I had to use the word *magic* to describe this. There was no better word.

The more this happened, the more I started to expect magic. It was no different than expecting the sun to rise in the morning. It became my new normal.

But here's the thing . . .

You don't have to wait for life to show you magic. In fact, go all in on loving yourself and then, expect magic. When you look for it, it will find you. But it helps to notice it when it starts, rather than chalk it off to coincidence or worse, pay no attention.

Life rewards you more when you pay attention to its gifts. Cliché as this sounds, I've found it to be true. Our attention is like a spotlight in the darkness. What we focus on becomes our experience of reality. Simply put: what you expect, you receive.

Want to take this to the next level? Then feel grateful when you experience magic. Want to take it even higher? Feel grateful *before* you experience magic, just expecting it. Then watch life pour it on you. I'm not saying this because it sounds good. It really works. Just try it.

None of this is rocket science. If you've lived life, I'm willing to bet you've experienced the same. So, *if* you loved yourself truly and deeply, what would you do?

Me, I'd expect magic and feel grateful for it. I hope you do the same.

ONE LAST THING . . .

When I came up with the Love Yourself practice, it was an attempt to save myself. I'm so fortunate that it worked. But what I didn't expect was the rebirth it gave me. How it transformed my life.

Look, life is short enough. We are but a brief flash of light, and then we're gone. During our time here, we only have one job: to shine brilliantly. I say that because you exist, you *must* shine.

Do it for yourself. Do it for the sheer experience of it. Do it for the ones you love. Do it for whatever you believe in, but just do it. And when you love yourself, you naturally shine.

So use this manual to love yourself truly and deeply. If you fall short, so what? You're human. Get up, dust yourself off, and love yourself even more. In return, life will.

PART III

THE LESSON

INTRO

Six years after learning to love myself, I fell. The fault, purely mine.

I'd spent the previous two years coasting, focusing on problems, reacting to life rather than being proactive from the inside out. Eventually, the practice became an afterthought. I couldn't remember the last time I'd made the vow, let alone gone all in.

The self-love grooves I'd built were strong enough to run the show for a while. But the grooves of the past run deep. Slack off long enough, water flows down those channels again.

My mind started to show the results. Then, my life. Yet, I coasted. Laziness has its own momentum. And the longer I coasted, the more I avoided what I needed most. The ego is tricky that way.

Then, an unexpected breakup with a woman I loved dearly. I fell hard.

Here's the good thing about falling: your ego drops faster than you. So it's easy to give it up. And I did. The shame of letting this happen, of being the one person who should have known better, of not living what I literally wrote a book about. I had to save myself, so I gave it all up.

I returned to the practice. Brick by brick, pathway by pathway, groove by groove. Loving myself all over again. But often, even though I knew what the next step was, I fought it. Truth be told, I was punishing myself for failing this badly.

Despite my resistance, despite making it harder than it needed to be, despite getting in my own way, the practice still worked. In less than a month, I was transformed. Loving yourself works, period.

This section, "The Lesson," is that deeply personal story. Every single word, like the rest of the book, is true. My biggest weakness, and one many readers have shared with me as well, is that once things get good, I start to coast. I'm sharing this experience with you so that you don't.

You'll see me fall, claw my way up, and then rise using the same principles that once saved my life. You'll also understand the nuances of the journey. I believe that these will help you.

Sometimes, we learn more from the mistakes of others than their successes. Don't be surprised if you find this to be the most useful section of the book.

I

I come home on a red-eye. I could have taken an easier flight but I wanted to return to her. I've been away a week and a half. On the ride into the city, I watch glass buildings in the financial district glow under the morning sun. I smile.

I open the door, she comes and hugs me. But not the way she normally does, where it's a run to me and holding tight. She leans into me, her grip weak.

"What's wrong?" I ask.

She's been up all night, crying. She's leaving me. She needs time and space. Not ready for commitment. Doesn't desire me. Doesn't feel for me the way I do for her. *It's not you*, she says, *it's me*.

The world spins. Like I'd walked in, stepped on a rug, and she bent down and ripped it off the floor. There I am, feet in the air, falling backward, slow motion. No control. And I can feel it. The floor inching closer and closer and I know that when I hit it, I will shatter.

A few days later, we make love. It is the most awkward of dances, knowing that the music's stopped. When I'm close, she asks me not to come inside of her. It's the first time she's ever done that.

I lie awake that night, my thoughts a mush, and I think to myself that if everything matters, this matters. She and I matter. Us matters. But if nothing matters, then neither does this.

Perhaps there is wisdom in this. If nothing matters in this play called life, best to exit stage left.

II

Next night, I fantasize about breaking into a friend's apartment while he's out of town, grabbing his handgun from the glass case, slapping it together. Clip in, safety off. Barrel under my jaw, squeeze the trigger. Done.

Would I shut my eyes at the moment or leave them open? That's the question that keeps me up. That's the thought I fall asleep to. In the morning, I wake up remembering how I used to be. The magic. Something inside me says, *Return to what works*.

I shove it aside.

III

It is evening. I have dinner with friends that I almost cancel because I don't want to talk, but in the end, I go.

I haven't seen them in forever and I love them. I take the six train uptown, listening to random motivational videos. Best to smother my mind with the opposite of my thoughts.

On one video, the speaker says, "There is only one choice, you must be the greatest you." He's got the southern twang of a preacher. "Write it down and declare it as a decree multiple times a day."

A decree. So old-fashioned. Hear ye, hear ye . . . I hereby decree that I will be the greatest me.

Just the thought makes me stand straighter.

IV

"Here's the good news," I say to her three days after rug flip. "I will die. You will die. The sun will eventually burn out, the moon will stop shining, and the earth will be a dull lifeless rock."

Pause for effect.

"The good news . . . none of this will have mattered."

Later, I realize what happens when you don't care about anything. You become fearless of sorts. Not so bad. Then

I flash to my friend's handgun and figure that this version of fearless isn't probably the best.

Here's the rub about emotional pain—it's a real thing. You lose yourself in it. You could be tying your laces, and the next thing you know, all you have is memories and images and jumbled thoughts flashing through your mind. Like a train whirling by while you stand on the platform, feeling the blast of the wind. Except here, the wind is like a slash, cutting and slicing.

"Return to your present," my friends told me over dinner. "Pain is when you're in the future in your head."

I'd been telling them what she'd said that day, about the men she wanted to date after me. Then, I switched the subject to what I might do. Go off to Mexico or somewhere, drop off the grid for a while. My friends are a long-married couple, Cheryl and Michael. They smiled.

"One day at a time, honey," she said. Cheryl Richardson, one of the wisest women I've ever met. "When you go to the future in your mind, just put your hand over your heart and say to yourself, 'I return to this. I return to this.'"

I haven't tried it yet, but I know I will. I have to.

V

I try it. It's been a week since rug flip. I put my hand over my heart, feel it beat, and repeat, "I return to this." Within a few seconds, I've changed the phrase and instead am saying, "I return to me. I return to me."

Later, in the shower, I close my eyes under the water and the train whooshes by. An anger rises within. Hand over my heart, *thump thump . . . thump thump*, I say to myself, "I return to me, I return to me."

And for that brief moment, the train disappears.

VI

It's day eight after rug flip. She hasn't moved out yet. It's the Christmas holidays and difficult to find a place last minute.

After I shower and get dressed, I take my mousse to her and ask, "Can you?" It's a ritual we had. She'd gently rub the foam in my hair, styling it, and I'd close my eyes and smile and feel so loved.

She takes the can and does this while I stare into her eyes. *I'm going to face this*, I think. *I will not run away.* I stare at her and when she finishes, she kisses me softly.

Tomorrow, I'm getting a haircut, so won't need this. The day after, I will fly to San Francisco to see family. It hits me that today could have been the last time we ever do this.

VII

My friend James calls and says that he'll keep his ringer on at night.

"I never do that," he says, "but I want you to know that it's on for you."

I've watched him go from heartache to heartache since I've known him. But the trend is this: he falls up. It's impressive. After each breakup, he does his daily practice hard. Eventually, his life is better than it ever was before.

His daily practice is this: physical, mental, emotional, spiritual. I will do this. I've seen it work wonders for him.

For physical, I will work out every other day and eat clean and healthy. No alcohol, it's a depressant.

For mental, I will write daily. I will take this pain and energy and create something from it. Also, at work, each day I will take the thing I've been putting off the most and get that done. This will move me forward.

For emotional, I will spend quality time with at least one person a day. This will make me get out of my head.

For spiritual, whenever I catch myself in my head, spinning and falling, I'll put my hand over my heart and return to myself.

At night, lying in bed, I say to her, "You're in luck."

"Why?"

It's pathetic and whiny and I hate saying it but I do it anyway. "Because you only have one more night of this."

"Don't say things like this," she says.

"Don't do things like this," I say.

She grows quiet. I lie in darkness, head spinning, and I place my hand on my heart and softly, I say to myself, "I return to me. I return to me. I return to me . . ."

VIII

It's the day before my flight. She's found a place and will move out while I'm in San Francisco. I wake up wishing this day didn't exist, that I could just wipe it away.

While she's out, I call Cheryl.

"I need you to remind me of truths," I say.

She toured with Oprah for a year. Wise doesn't even begin to describe her. She has a level of seeing what is real that's unparalleled, and I desperately need that.

"Heartbreak triggers old abandonment," she says. "It's the little child who experienced it—and we all do—and is terrified. At that age, your parents are everything, and the sense of abandonment means death."

This stops me. I feel like it's me that's suffering, not a long-forgotten child. But what she says, even if it's a tiny fraction of this, it rings right.

"Your child needs to know that it can trust you. That you got it. That is what you must do. Each moment it hurts bad, each time you create dramatic thoughts about the future, go to your heart. Place your hand there and tell it, 'I got you.' That's all it needs."

When I get off the phone, I do it. *I got you, you can trust me. I got you. I got you.*

I go to the gym. I see a man working out hard and say to him, "Impressive."

We've run into each other before, just never talked. He comes over, grins, and pulls out his phone to the gym's website.

"Look," he says. "That's me."

He's the highlighted member of the month. On the left, photo of an out-of-shape guy. On the right, present-day him, muscled.

"Impressive," I say again.

"Transformation takes work," he says.

I stare at him stupidly. "Can you repeat that?"

"Transformation, it takes work."

"Quote of the week, man," I say to him. "Quote of the week."

When I spoke with Cheryl earlier, she said, "You have one of the best hearts on the planet."

I took it in. What's it gonna take for me to believe it? Does God have to part the heavens and smack boom it down to me? Or a deathbed realization?

To be reborn, you must die first. And this sure feels like death. I'm done downplaying what those I respect see in me.

"Protect your heart," she said. "Give it what it needs."

I will. No matter what it takes. I will.

IX

The problem with heartbreak is that it feels like it will never end. You're plummeted by emotions and memories and projections and just when you're strung out, another wave smacks into you. It goes on and on.

She returns from her errands, hugs me.

"My love," I say. Something we always called each other.

She steps back and smiles, quiet. That's enough. Ripping this Band-Aid off will hurt, but I must do it.

I tell her what Cheryl said about my heart. Then I say, "I need to save this heart. I don't know how or if I'll be able to, but I need to save it."

She nods. I know she loves me, but her mind is set.

"I'm going out," I say. I have a haircut at five. "I'll be back by six. I want you to leave and not be here when I come back. Because when I return, I need to feel and write and pack and face this heartbreak."

The color on her face shifts.

"I fly out tomorrow morning, you can come back then. And when you move your stuff out, don't leave me anything. No note, no gifts, no record of us. Nothing."

I can tell she wasn't expecting this.

"I know the lessons you think you're gonna learn," I say. "And I also know a couple other lessons you'll learn that you didn't want to. That's yours. Saving my heart, it's my responsibility."

I stand close, stare deep into her.

"This is a man who would have stood by your side all your life. You have no idea what love is." Then, I can't help myself. "If you decide that this is the heart you want, then reach out."

Neither of us blinks.

"Last thing," I say. "It's the only thing I really ask of you. Wear your helmet."

She loves biking in the city and I always bugged her to wear a helmet. I still love her deeply. Nothing's changed for me except one thing: I'm going to save myself.

I grab a jacket and walk out, not looking back. I take the stairs, rather than waiting for the elevator. They lead me to the basement and I have to walk up to the third floor and take the elevator down, making me feel a little foolish, but I don't care.

I walk out into the evening, walking straighter than I have in a while.

X

"You're a magnificent man," Cheryl once told me. It blew my mind that someone I admired and respected so much thought that of me. I wish I'd believed her down to my core.

I decide that I will create a file, put in every sincere compliment I receive, and then repeat it to myself as truth. It is a gift that others have given me. If they see me as this, what right do I have to not see it in myself?

So, I start the list:

1. I am a magnificent man.
2. I have one of the best hearts on the planet.

XI

I return at 6:16 p.m. In the elevator, I find myself hoping that she stayed. For whatever reason, even if it was for a better goodbye, but as I walk to my apartment, hope evaporates and I know.

I open the door to a dark apartment. She left a candle lit by the window. If it wasn't for the circumstances, I would enjoy the ambiance. I storm in, blow the candle out, and scream at the ceiling. Every single piece of me wants to explode.

Then I lie on the couch and stare at the walls in a stupor until I doze off. When I wake up, I change the home screen photo on my phone. It used to be one of her, staring into the camera, her face tilted, smiling.

I replace it with a lotus opening to the morning sun.

Then, I mindlessly scroll through Twitter until I stop at a photo posted by Dwayne Johnson, The Rock. It's one of his infamous early morning workouts. Sweaty, grimacing, he's going full-out on the loaded squat bar.

This is a man who, in his early twenties, was cut from the Canadian Football League. His dreams of going on to a career in the NFL, dashed. On that long ride home in his father's pickup truck, he leafed through his wallet to find seven dollars to his name.

He sat around in his parents' apartment for two weeks, feeling sorry for himself. Then, he was done. Time to reinvent himself.

He went into professional wrestling, starting from scratch, and gave it everything he had. The result: one of the most successful careers in professional wrestling, ever. At the height of his fame, he left to become an actor.

Each time he reinvented himself, he used the same playbook: he committed, he went all in. After his early movies failed and he was written off, he still stayed true to his vision.

Today, he's a blockbuster movie star. His movies consistently break records all over the world. And the name of his film studio: Seven Bucks Productions.

I scroll through his feed. Photos of him with fans, photos of him on set, photos of him working out. Always grinning. He's devoted to his wife and daughters. His work ethic is legendary. He's had rough patches, but he's always pulled himself up.

I read a quote of his: "If I give you my word to get something done—it gets done."

It's obvious that this doesn't just apply to others, he keeps his word to himself. He lives a level of excellence that's rare.

Something I've learned: to grow fast, find someone you admire, and then model whatever it is about them that inspires you.

Excellence will be my model. That is what I want out of this.

"Be excellent," I say to myself, my voice hollow in the dark apartment.

At this moment, it seems so far away. But at least I have something to shoot for.

XII

At the airport, about to drop off my checked bag, I freeze. I don't want to go, something inside begs. I don't want to go. I don't want to go. Like a little child, it begs and begs, terrified. All around me, passengers and crew rush to catch their flights, living their lives, dancing their dance. Nothing matters.

But what will I do? Run home and beg her to stay? When, in the history of mankind, has that ever worked? Besides, I don't want her to be with me out of guilt or pleading, but because her heart wants mine. If she wants her freedom and I love her, let her have it.

I've lived enough to know that life gets uncomfortable when you try to force it through the pinhole of your desires. I must remove myself from this. Whether it's because I have no choice or simply because I must save myself.

I drop the bag off and then sit at the gate, waiting for my flight to board.

At this moment, alone in a crowded airport, I once again remember the way I used to be. The magic I felt. The sureness of having figured out how life worked. And yet, here I am, miserable and not living what I wrote about. Disgusted with myself for having fallen this far.

XIII

I almost miss my flight. Turns out that they changed gates and I zoned out through the announcement. By the time I wonder why no one is boarding, it's almost time to depart.

I check the monitor, then walk fast to the new gate. But I do not run. There is a part of me that would be just fine with missing the flight. Chalk it up to the Universe, then.

No such luck. I get there in time, board, and pass out in my seat before takeoff. When I wake up, the wing is skimming clouds and the land far below is covered in snow. I pass out again for a while and wake to the sound of the loudest baby in the world. It's laughing, crying, screaming. No more sleep.

I think about her. I know I could run away and find myself in the arms of another. Or ten others. Rarely works. That's what happened with us. She ended a marriage and I was the next stop.

"Statistically," James said when he saw me, "the odds were against you."

I'm not dumb. I know these things. But when did statistics ever guide the human heart?

I fell for her hard, and she for me. We were close friends for two years, then together for almost a year. "You're my greatest love," she told me. "You can trust my love, I want you to relax fully into it." All this right before I left for my trip. The one from which I returned to rug-flip day. Afterward, she admitted that perhaps I'd just been safety for her.

Gazing out at the open sky, I'm still stunned by how quickly something that once felt so tight can unwind. The baby laughs on and on.

I escape to the restroom. While I'm washing my hands, I stare at myself in the mirror, deep into my eyes. Next thing I know, I'm whispering, "I love myself, I love myself, I love myself."

I repeat it again and again until it takes over my mind.

XIV

When I return to my seat, something inside me is calmer.

I think of my friend's handgun. So many ways to exit stage left. To unwind my life in an instant. The captain announces the descent. In that moment, I decide that I will do "the mirror" every chance I get.

The plane is close to landing. It's too late to go back to the restroom. So, hand over my heart, I look down at the browned winter hills of Northern California and say to myself, *I love myself, I love myself, I love myself* . . .

XV

I land, grab an Uber. Feels strange while the car weaves through San Francisco. This was once home, memories. Today, it's a place I visit.

I call and she picks up. I tell her what I feel. That I love her fully. I want her. I want to create something beautiful from this place, together. She's crying, saying that this is hard for her and imagines that it could be harder for me.

I don't respond to it. My suffering will only make hers worse. I just repeat who she is to me and that I want her. No pleading, just truth.

"I'm sorry," she says, "but I need to do this."

There is no argument against that. Nor will I ever argue with her to stay. I want her to come to me with her heart. She knows that.

"I want you to take care of yourself," she says.

When the conversation's over, I stare blankly out to the Bay and then the Uber drops me off at the apartment where I'll be staying. It's almost empty, the occupants having moved out recently. The plants left behind are dead. Fits how I feel.

If I try to figure out her reasons, I feel pain. If I think of where she'll be in the future, I feel pain. If I think of where I was with her in the past, pain. If I think of being without her, guess what, more pain.

The future equals pain. The past equals pain. So I must return to the present and give myself love. Every chance I get.

I stand by the window, stare out at the infamous rust-colored bridge, put my hand on my heart, and desperately try to love myself the way I know how. I repeat it to myself.

XVI

I shower and go to my brother's birthday party. It's the reason I'm in San Francisco. I was going to skip it, tired from all the traveling before this trip, but she's moving out and this gives her space and keeps me from going insane watching her do it.

Everyone's here. My mother beaming with pride whenever she stands next to me and my brother. Her boys.

"Look at this place, Mom," I say, putting my arm around her. This is one of the nicest houses I've ever been in. And I still remember being a child, when we were on the streets, nowhere to go.

"All thanks to you, Mom," I say.

Before she can respond, I kiss her on the head and walk away. If we spend more time together, she'll sense my pain and ask. I don't want to put that on her. Sometimes,

I think that a mother feels her child's pain more acutely than the child itself.

For the rest of the evening, when anyone asks where my woman is, I dodge and deflect. For a few, I state what's happening, but I don't let the conversation go further. I'm firm, my game face on.

With one, I can't. Aniela Gregorek. She and her husband, Jerzy, fled the communist state in Poland and have been together for over forty years. Both are Olympic weight-lifting trainers who coach celebrity clients. Both also write poetry, the kind of clear and honest lines you get from those who've lived through oppression and fought for their lives.

"I see the sadness in your eyes," she says.

I almost lose it, but catch myself. This is a celebration, not a pity party. I tell her what happened. She smiles gently and puts her hand over my heart.

"That is your gift," she says. "You keep this open."

I'm trying my very hardest not to devolve in front of everyone.

"It's hard," I say, "and it hurts so bad."

She pulls me close, holds me for a long while. When I step back, her eyes are moist.

"Are you writing?" she asks.

I nod, yes.

"Good. Transform this into the page. It will help others."

XVII

As the party winds down, I chat with Tabreez, a sweet guy I've met before. He tells me what he's learning from other leaders—the way we look at life.

The first: **life happens to me**. This is the place we normally live from, especially as a victim.

The second: **life happens for me**. This upends everything. You look for the good that life is giving you, including the lessons.

The third: **life happens through me**. Where you flow with life and don't even have to look for the good because you're experiencing it.

The man came out of nowhere and handed me a gift all wrapped up with a shiny bow. I couldn't have asked for it—I had no idea what I needed. But here it is. A map. Point A to Point B to Point C. How to go from victim to magic. All I have to do is shift my mind.

XVIII

I wake up the next morning and stare out at the view. A tanker lazily making its way across San Francisco Bay. Blue sky, birds everywhere. The bridge is beautiful.

I realize that the plants I thought were dead might not be. They're just dry and barren. Nature fighting to live. So I take the one cup I have in this apartment and water them. While I'm here, I'm going to give them love.

XIX

I must stay true to my commitment to work out every other day. So I call the local gyms, find one willing to sell me a temporary pass for the holidays, and head over.

Alex, the membership guy, tries to chitchat while setting me up. *Do I want to sign up for a package?* Not interested. *A personal training special?* Not interested.

"I just want to lift heavy things, man," I say to him.

He wants to show me where the classes and studios are.

"Just the heavy stuff," I say. "That's all I want to see."

He gives the shortest tour of his life. I check out the squat rack and make sure the dumbbells go high enough, that's it. I sign up.

I do my workout, but slightly different, thanks to Aniela. Last night, when I told her my current routine of compound movements only, she suggested waiting longer between sets.

"You're not working hard enough if you don't need much rest."

I was used to resting less than a minute. Anything beyond that and I got bored. I wasn't in the gym to sit around. I wanted to move the weight, push myself.

"That is endurance," she said. "Push harder, rest longer, three minutes between sets. The body needs to reset to push hard again. That is power."

That last part caught my attention. "I'll try it."

So I do. And it's amazing. I push heavier weight, better form, and by the time I'm done, my body feels different than before. I can feel my muscles reeling from the assault.

Sometimes, it's good to know that you're not just a head floating around. You're a physical being. How you do this is by pushing your body. And even if it's just for those moments, it snaps you out of your thoughts.

I step out. It's raining and umbrellas are in full bloom. I lift my head up to the sky and feel the water on my face.

XX

I've been thinking about death. Surprise surprise. The thing about death is the finality of it. A sharp blade that slices through life, cutting off whoever that's gone. There's no talking with them, no making amends, no saying the things unsaid. They're gone and that's that.

A while ago, I tried meditating on death each morning. I'd read that the samurai would do this, making them fearless in battle. I did it for a while, grew lazy, and stopped. I had no battles to ride into. My days were too safe.

But I sit in the empty apartment at night and realize that safety is an illusion. It is the biggest grandest illusion ever pulled off. There is one thing that is real and that is death. He stands in front of me, just a step away.

Each moment I live, I step toward death. Death smiles, steps back. I step forward, death back one step. Me forward, death back, me forward, death back. Step step step. And then, I step forward and death doesn't move. I am his.

I look out at the moon. It's huge tonight and lights up the Bay. If my heart stopped this moment and I dropped, the life squeezing out of me and my vision tunneling into a pinhole, would I be remembering rug-flip day and how much it hurt or would I grasp at the moon one last time and think how beautiful it is?

XXI

While walking around town, I come across a cryotherapy place. I've never done it, but been meaning to, so I go inside. Next thing I know, I'm standing in my underwear in a cylindrical tube filling with nitrogen-cooled air.

"How was it?" the attendant asks when I step out.

"Not bad," I say. It was only three minutes. "My stomach hurts a little, though."

"That's because the body pools blood to your organs. It's trying to survive."

When you stress the body, it responds. First, survival mode and blood flows to vital organs. But as the stress passes, it adapts. It has no choice, it's built that way. Lifting heavy in the gym is the best example. Your muscles respond by getting stronger. Perhaps it's the same with the mind.

Mine is in survival mode. But as it adapts, it will grow stronger and I will be better. I just have to keep at it. No matter what thoughts come or what I return to once she's moved out, no matter what. Day by day. Just move the damn weight.

XXII

Foggy morning in San Francisco. Day before Christmas, the streets almost empty. My mind keeps going to the what-ifs. What if I'd been this way? Or that way? What if I'd done this or that? What if on rug-flip day, I'd been stronger, what if, what if?

That is poison, I realize, watching a lone jogger in the drizzle. And there is no truth there. The truth is this: what is.

What is is what happened. There is not one single thing I can do about it. It is the past. And the past is dead. Done. The only question is, Who am I going to be today? That's it.

XXIII

It's raining hard. I watch from the living room windows. The trees in San Francisco are still green in the winter. My thoughts are a jumble. I remember the map—*to* me to *through* me. I need to shift my mind.

I return to a habit: ten breaths to love myself. Each time my mind is caught in past, future, or what-if, I will take ten deep and full breaths. With each inhale, I will tell myself, *I love myself*. Whenever I can, I will make myself feel it. That's it.

But . . .

If my mind stutters and returns to the jumble, I will reset the counter, start again. Even if it takes a hundred breaths to reach ten uninterrupted breaths, I will do this. Each time.

I will go for excellence in my thoughts, I tell myself. I do this for a day. It's difficult, but I do it. But at night, I devolve.

Pain hits hardest at night. We were happy. We loved each other. How could this be happening? I try switching to loving myself but it's next to impossible. The pain is physical and real in my chest.

So I let it be. I tell the pain: *Come if you wish, I will face you*. And it does. It churns through me, wrings me out, and when it passes, I am still there. Then, I do the ten breaths.

XXIV

Yes, rug flip happened. Yes, I flew back, the floor coming up, knowing that once I hit it, I would shatter. But I haven't hit it yet.

I don't have to continue falling. I don't have to shatter. It is a choice.

Remember this: you are more powerful than your illusions.

XXV

I close my eyes and feel the fire consuming me, burning away all that's not.

XXVI

I once asked a monk how he found peace.

"I say yes," he said. "To all that happens, I say yes."

The last thing my mind wants to do is say yes. It's stuck in the what-ifs, what I should have done, replaying the past, sometimes playing a stronger version of me, other times showing how pathetic I was.

My mind is screaming one loud NO at life.

But I need to say yes. To what is. All of it. If I wish to be in my power, I have no choice. Otherwise, I stay a victim.

XXVII

She calls me on Christmas afternoon.

"I just saw your message," she says.

The message she's referring to is a text I sent this morning.

"This is hard, my love," I'd written, "really really hard."

"I saw your message," she says again, "and I feel bad."

"Not the intention," I say. "It was a moment of weakness."

"Are you taking care of yourself?"

"I'm being me," I say. "I'm writing, I'm exercising, I'm staring at the sky and thinking."

A bit of small talk, then she says, "There is a part of me that wants to spend my time loving you, but this feels right. I need time and space."

"Then I must support it," I say. "I love you. So I can only give you what you need."

I'm realizing that this is hard on her as well. No need to create stories about her that serve neither of us. I will not cheapen the love we had. I'll just be me. And in the meantime, if she is incapable of loving or saving me, I will save myself. I will love myself.

XXVIII

So, life for you. How do you get there?

You decide that you're not a random leaf twisting in the fall wind. There is a pattern to things, something bigger than you. Doesn't matter if you have proof or not, you decide that this is the way it is.

Then, look for what's working, what you have, what you should be grateful for if you weren't so caught up in your mind. Doesn't matter if it's minor or major. The act shifts you from what you've lost to what you have and what you're gaining.

I do this. I list all that I have. The Christmas greetings on my phone from so many who love me. Then, what I'm gaining. I'm focusing on my body and mind in a way that I haven't in a long while. Heck, all these days of no appetite have made my abs their best in years.

Suddenly, I laugh. I'd been complaining for months about needing a writing retreat. Except I didn't know where I'd go and what I'd write about. Well, problem solved.

There is good happening here. I'm not sure where it's going, which makes it difficult, and that's where the trust in life comes in. Just lift the weight.

Feeling slightly better, I walk to the Marina Green. The gym is closed and I need to move my body. So I do sprints. I haven't done them in years. I do them so hard that several runners pause to watch me throttle by.

Finished, struggling for breath, I stare at the sunset over the bridge. Finally, I gasp out the only two words that come: thank you.

I repeat them to whatever the Bigger Than Me is. Thank you. Thank you. Thank you.

XXIX

Mornings are hard. I wake up to the cold stark reality
of what is and my mind immediately jumps into the
what-ifs. So I go to the ten breaths. I do them with a
desperation.

When mammals breathe, they take in life-giving oxygen
and release toxic carbon dioxide. I'm doing the same.
With each in-breath, I say to myself: *I love myself*. With
each out-breath, I release whatever's inside.

I've started imagining light flowing into me from above
with each in-breath.

Death is still on my mind. There he is, beckoning with
that bony finger. Breath by breath, I step forward. He
steps back. There is only one guarantee: at some point,
one breath will be my last.

This morning, staring out at the Bay, I hope it will be one
of love.

XXX

The hallmark of a victim is that you make it about you.
"This happened to me." "She did it to me." And so on.

What about her? Everyone has their reasons and pain, known and unknown. This is also happening to her. Who I'm being to her is what I'm doing to her. And who I'm being to me is what I'm doing to me.

It's up to me to stop this. I can't control or be responsible for another's mind and actions. Only mine. So I must work on myself. I have the map.

Instead of something happening to me, make it this: I happen to *it*.

Choose who I am. Choose to come from a place of power. From a place of loving myself truly and deeply. That is happening to it. See what results.

XXXI

I start meditating. Something I haven't done seriously in over a year. I put on a piece of music that makes me feel good. With each breath, I feel light enter my body from above and I say to myself, *I love myself*. Then I breathe out whatever needs to go. All the carbon dioxide of the mind.

The mind wanders, of course, but the music becomes the anchor, subtly reminding me of what I'm doing and as it winds to a close, that time is running out. That naturally relaxes my mind. It desperately wants this peace too.

This meditation centers me more than anything else. It is special, by me, purely for me.

XXXII

My father beat my mother and when I'd try to fight him, he'd turn on me until my face was bloody and she begged him to stop. After we left him, I was molested. Bullied? I could write a textbook.

Did all this make me a victim? Perhaps.

But I'm no longer a child. And an adult only gets two choices: victim or hero.

Long time ago, I made the choice to be the latter. I joined the army, I strengthened my body, I learned martial arts. My childhood molded me into the fiercely loyal man that I am. It gave me the sensitivity and depth to write the books that I do.

I'm damn proud of that boy who survived to be this man. He took what happened and created good out of it. He became the hero of that story.

Time to step up, make the choice again. Be the hero of this story.

XXXIII

If a person or situation exits your life, it doesn't change who you are. Only you know you. And if you're unhappy with any aspect of yourself, then use this emotional energy. Wring out every single fiber. It no longer happens to you. *You* happen to it.

Burn into the Phoenix. Go all in. Become excellent.

Or, as I've started asking myself lately, *What would The Rock do?*

XXXIV

The ten breaths are becoming more natural. I find myself feeling better. Whenever I pass a mirror, whether in the bathroom or the gym, I walk right up to it and stare into my eyes and feel love for myself. I'm even standing taller, my head high.

Not all the time, though. What-ifs zing at me repeatedly. They are my insecurities, popping up, dressed as projections of her without me. Telling me that I wasn't good enough.

Fears, all of them. Hallucinated snakes dangling from the ceiling.

Not useful, I tell myself. Not real. The only thing that is real is what is. And what is is that I'm all in on becoming excellent. And no matter where she goes, she's going to miss out on my excellent self.

At least my sense of humor is starting to return.

But even though I can almost imagine a future where I'll continue getting better, there's a stumbling block ahead. Once things get good, I'll get comfortable and coast. I've done that many times in my life.

Not this time. Excellence does not coast.

My greatest strength is my belief in the power of commitment. Every substantial achievement in my life is a result of this. I will eventually have to use it here.

XXXV

A friend texts, offering a guys' trip in January. I know what that means: parties and women. So I ask myself: *If I loved myself, what would I do?*

The answer is clear. Distractions feed emptiness and my heart needs to heal. I pass.

This question returned to me during meditation, and I've started using it regularly. The best part is the *if*. It's perfect for those moments where I'm not exactly loving myself. I still get the answer I would if I did.

So simple. So effective. The best things are.

XXXVI

A thought zings by: I needed this.

I'd been adrift for a long while, not pushing myself, mainly coasting. Not anymore. It's like I've been slapped awake. I feel raw and real in a way I haven't before. Each day is marked by an intense focus on loving myself. To be excellent.

The thought doesn't last long. But still, it feels damn good.

XXXVII

The mind can only hold one thought at a time. And each time I repeat a thought with emotion, I reinforce it, increasing the chance that it will return. So my future thoughts and emotions are up to me. I'm laying the tracks down for them in this moment.

I tilt my face to the sun, close my eyes, and feel light clear away all that's not. And all that time, I say to myself: *I love myself. I love myself. I love myself.*

Why light? Because light is life. Ask any plant.

Even at night or when meditating, I feel the light. I imagine stars and galaxies flowing down to me and through me. Light is always available. It's becoming a core part of loving myself.

My name, in the language it was given, means Lotus. A flower that rises through the muck and opens to the light. And then, according to the ancient stories, God rests in the petals.

Light opens me, it heals me, it frees me. All I have to do is receive it.

XXXVIII

Morning. The alarm goes off. I come out of a dream, the mind already starting its pain and what-if routine, and I do the ten breaths. Slowly and deeply. Instead of the mind wreaking havoc, I'm imposing my will on it. I'm in charge, laying down the tracks, deepening the grooves. This is excellence in my thoughts.

Next, I grab a coffee and meditate. It opens me to the light like nothing else. By the time the music ends, something inside me is settled.

The rest of the day is moment by moment. I write with an energy I've never had before. When I go to the gym or do sprints, I push hard and rest long in between. It makes me feel like a physical animal.

Where the head goes, the body follows. But vice versa as well. A solution here.

XXXIX

A friend randomly texts me. We haven't spoken in months.

"How's your health?"

Half a year ago, I'd told him a bare-bones version of an issue I'd been dealing with—a concussion that resulted in months of debilitating pain, then recurring headaches. Nothing beyond that, my ego kept me from going deeper.

But if anything must shatter, it should be my ego. It keeps me from being real. It keeps me from accepting the help that life offers. I call and fill him in on it.

"Funny," he says when I'm done. "This morning, I thought of how you can fix this. That's why I texted."

He's a master at optimizing his health. I can see a light at the end of the tunnel.

"I will help you," he says. "Let's gather all the test results and set up a plan. We'll do it week by week. The good thing, I know that you'll actually implement it."

He knows my belief in the power of commitment. Once I'm in, I'm all in. Both a strength and a weakness in relationships, as I'm painfully learning. One should earn my loyalty, not just receive it because I love them. But forget relationships. Forget her. She is not saving me. I will.

XL

Am I angry? Of course I am. At her. At what happened. At myself. At life.

Why couldn't you just let me be happy? I beg life in my head. *Why couldn't you make me grow like this when we were together?* Or, the one that plagues me the most, *How could this have happened?*

Life doesn't answer. Or perhaps, if it does, I'm shouting too loud to listen.

Anger only destroys me. So whenever I feel anger or despair—and there are moments throughout the day— I return to the ten breaths.

Besides, I cannot let this diminish who I am. I'm an openhearted, loving man, and that's that. In this is power. And no matter what, I will not cheapen my love for her by rationalizing it away. Love is what it is. It takes strength to continue loving the person who hurt you. There is zero weakness in this.

Whenever anger or pain comes, I will let it wash over me, and once it's passed, I'll still be there, standing. Being me. Then, I will shift to the light.

XLI

I go see Jerzy and he trains me. This is next-level stuff, Olympic weight lifting. Power, in this case, is the greatest amount of work you can do in the shortest amount of time. Cleans and snatches demand everything your body's got. Such power transforms the body. I can feel my internal systems waking up, coming online.

It's the same with the mind. I could spread out what I'm doing to love myself over months. A little bit here, little bit there, or only when I feel like it or have the strength. But that's endurance. And who wants to just endure life?

Besides, it wouldn't get me this progress I'm feeling. I know it down to my core. The same solution applies for both body and mind: dive in, give it all you got.

"I'll tell you my philosophy," Jerzy says after the session. "One word: improve."

That rings true with where I am.

"If you want to see anyone's philosophy," he says, "look at their life. We are all living our philosophy. Our life is the result."

XLII

If I could float above the earth and watch history unfold, all the human drama from the past to the present spinning by, and then zoom down to the physical me, sitting there in pain, what would I say?

Would I say, "Go ahead, suffer away"? Doubt it.

I would be gentle with myself. I would look into my eyes with deep love and say, "It's okay. Let go. Wish her the best, wish her good, and let go. Be in the light and trust in life."

XLIII

After Jerzy and Aniela fled Poland, they landed in New York City with practically no money. First day, their luggage was stolen. But they had their priorities. They had to find a gym and go train.

They went to the Salvation Army, found clothes, but the only pair of sneakers that fit Jerzy were bright pink.

"They were a dollar," he says, laughing. "I had no choice. I had to buy them."

At the gym, the rack was occupied by two large men, both lifting seriously heavy weight. But their form was wrong. Their backs were rounded, barely holding the weight up.

Trying to be helpful, Jerzy walked over and told them that they needed to fix their form. They looked at him, then down at his bright pink sneakers, and started laughing.

"So what to do," he says. "Sometimes, there is no telling. You just have to show."

He grabbed the loaded bar and did three perfect snatches. The same weight that had them sagging. After that, each time they saw Jerzy, they were his best friends.

Lesson one: never judge a man by his shoes.

Lesson two: if people doubt you, just be excellent.

XLIV

Moment of weakness, I text her. She texts me back. Blah blah blah you deserve the best blah blah blah.

I stare at it for a while, still amazed how after all that you've shared together, someone can change their behavior so quickly. But it's her thing, not mine. I will be me.

I pull out the list I started. I haven't added to it, except a comment from a friend.

I add hers to it.

1. I am a magnificent man.
2. I have one of the best hearts on the planet.
3. I look great.
4. I deserve the best.

This guy is starting to sound rather excellent.

XLV

I'm at dinner with family at a Shabu Shabu place on Lombard Street. It's a celebration of my nephew being born one hundred days ago. He's fast asleep in a baby carrier on his mom's chest. His older brother sits next to me, banging on his iPad with chopsticks.

"Being born is a terrible thing," my brother says. "There you are, nice and cozy in the womb, all your needs met. You have movement sometimes. There's music sometimes. You have all the food you want and suddenly, the walls start squeezing in and the water's gone. Gone. And you're pushed and squeezed out and there's all these lights and noise—"

"And they slap you," I say.

"Slap you. You were all perfect and content and now they're slapping you."

Everyone's laughing. He's in fine form tonight.

"No one wants to be born," he says, staring straight at me. "You gotta be pushed out."

The hundred-day-old man of the hour wakes up, taking everyone's attention.

My brother returns to me. "Joe's moving to LA."

Joe's a new-agey friend of my brother. Always positive and upbeat.

"It'll suit him," I say. San Francisco stopped being the bastion of love and openness long ago. Southern California is where it's at these days.

"Yeah," he says. "You'd be surprised, he's really smart. Guess what his background is?"

"Particle physics," I say. Probably the most outlandish thing I can think of.

"He was in the mob."

"You're kidding. Joe?"

"When he was nineteen. He was low-level, in and out of prison, but they noticed that he was smart so they said they'd send him to law school, and when he got out, he'd be the mob's lawyer."

"Lifetime employment," I say, laughing. "Not a job you quit."

"And he gets a girl pregnant. She decides to keep the baby. So Joe's son is born and he thinks his life is over.

He's gotta change, he can't have a son whose dad is in jail, so he left the mob."

That's a heck of a story. I can't even imagine Joe jaywalking, let alone in the mob.

"Sometimes," my brother says, "what you think is the worst thing that happened to you turns out to be the best thing that ever did."

XLVI

I'm not happy. I'm not smiling. In fact, I'm often miserable when missing her. But I am better. There's no denying it. It's only been a few weeks but I feel like a lifetime of gunk's been stripped away. I feel real for the first time in forever.

At moments, I wonder if life actually did me a favor. I sure am not asleep anymore. I have an intense focus on loving myself. My writing is flowing. My workouts are off the charts.

The Rock would approve.

XLVII

I'm on fire because I'm in survival mode. Eventually, I will
run out of steam and coast. It's human nature. It's my
nature. And no matter the progress I'm making, I'm still
in the minors. Soon, it will be time to step up to the big
leagues.

How do I get there? Commitment.

XLVIII

One of the best things about meditation is that insights
come. Answers to questions I didn't even know I had.
Here's one I got this morning: *The love I have for her is
pure and beautiful. Time to give myself this love.*

One has to be careful about these insights. The mind is
tricky, slipping in through back doors. What might seem
like an answer could just be the mind doing its thing. So
here's the way to solve that. Ask yourself: Is this fear or is
this love?

If fear, you know the answer. Not real, not useful,
hallucinated snake.

If love, then apply.

XLIX

I've noticed that things are starting to, well, just work.
Dealing with health issues? The right person texts out
of nowhere, offering to help. An encounter saves an
investment, one I would have lost otherwise. And so on.

Coincidences? Sure. Synchronicities? Why not. But
here's the thing: I decided to believe that I'm not a lone
leaf in the wind. I am part of something Bigger Than Me.
If that's the case, then this shouldn't surprise me one bit.

When you love yourself, life loves you too.

L

I haven't had a drop of alcohol. My social media
consumption is nil. Zero small-talk conversations.
Depressants, all of them. Carbon dioxide of the mind.

Pascal once said that humanity's problems stem from
man's inability to sit quietly in a room alone. Well, bring it
on, buddy. I got this.

Facing the fire strips away everything that's not. What's
left behind is the real me. And as much as my mind
wants to distract itself away, I will not let it. This is too
important. I am too important.

The thought that I'm too important catches me off guard. Only someone who loves themselves would think this. For the first time in what seems like eternity, I smile.

LI

I've been loving myself with a desperate intensity. To save myself. To get out of pain. To sidestep memories and projections of her. But what if rather than as a means to an end, loving myself is the end?

This would never have occurred to me when I first started. And even if it had, I wouldn't have been ready. But perhaps there are layers to loving myself, and I have to go through each to get to the next. Like a video game where you level up.

So I decide that I will love myself purely for myself. Not to survive. Not to heal. And not for her.

I will love myself because I am worthy of my own love.

LII

New Year's Eve. I go for a walk. It's a blustery night in San Francisco. As the walk winds down and I turn the corner to the apartment, I see an older African American couple taking photos of each other. He's wearing a parka. She's in a glittering black skirt, dressed to the nines.

"Want a photo together?" I ask.

She smiles huge. "Yes. That would be great."

She hands me the phone and snuggles into him. They hold each other the way that longtime lovers do. A sweet familiarity. I take four photos and for the last one, I say, "Give each other love."

He kisses her. She's beaming. I hand the phone back. They thank me and wish me a happy new year. I start to walk away, but for some reason I stop.

"I'm going through a heartbreak," I say. The wind whips silver across my eyes. "And it's . . . it's just nice to see love. So, thank you."

The woman puts her hands over her heart.

"Oh," she says with such kindness. "We will pray for you."

"Thank you." I'll take any help I can get.

I return to the dark apartment and head straight to my laptop and write this.

LIII

New Year's Day. Last time this year, I asked myself specific questions about what I wanted and wrote down the answers. Looking back, many of them came true. That is the power of deciding what you want and stating it clearly.

I'm starting to remember that life begins from the inside out. If I focus on what's within, the rest will resolve itself. So this year, I will do something different. Rather than goals to achieve, I will decide who I want to be. And then state that clearly.

I ask myself: *If I loved myself truly and deeply, who would I be?*

The answer is clear: I would be excellent.

Then I ask myself: *What would this require?*

Again, clear answer: Loving myself fiercely.

LIV

Try this out for a moment . . .

One: Your thoughts and emotions create your internal state.

Two: Your internal state influences your external state.

Three: Your external state affects your life.

So, if one leads to two, which leads to three: your thoughts and emotions directly affect your life.

Let's wind the clock back, see how this worked for me. After the head injury, I was living life from a place of protecting myself. Not pushing into anything. Being pulled along by events, rather than happening to them.

If that's my internal state, how will my life result?

If I was to be brutally honest—and I should, it's a gift to myself—I'd felt powerless since the injury. So how would this affect my life? Seeds grow where they're planted.

What's the lesson here?

Do whatever it takes to feel powerful from the inside out. To feel in control. To feel that I happen to things. Decide that I and only I am responsible for my feelings, my emotions, and ultimately, my life. Every single piece.

Whatever did happen, it happened, and that's that. Time to plant new seeds.

LV

So, how to plant new seeds? Simple. Start with the foundation: my thoughts and emotions. If anger, pain, jealousy, any form of fear—darkness, all. If love for myself, light. Be *that clear*. There is zero room for middle ground.

Shift to light every moment I can. Make myself feel it. Again and again. I've already been doing it, but take it up another notch. Not only am I planting seeds, I'm giving them the nourishment they need.

Loving myself is power. But it's not a onetime thing. Just like workouts, it must be done consistently, perhaps for as long as I live. But so what? If this is the solution, it's a damn good one. I am worth the magic that will result.

LVI

Time to grab the reins on my health. My friend who texted is putting together a program for me. But rather than waiting, I go visit Matt Cook, the best regenerative medicine physician in the country. Of all the doctors I saw last year, he's the only one who got me results.

We run through tests, showing that I've improved since I last saw him. Most importantly, my state of mind is proactive, rather than reactive. This helps with healing.

While there, I end up chatting with Lisa, a kind nurse who works hard, making sure all the patients are comfortable. But there is pain in her eyes. Her son died of a heroin overdose months ago.

I can't even imagine her pain. It would be like a forest fire compared to my matchstick. But it also reminds me of something: everyone knows pain. It may come in different forms or at different times. But it comes. It's a fundamental part of the human experience.

Pain doesn't make me unique. It makes me human. And no matter what I'm experiencing, I'm not alone. Plenty before me have been through it. As the Roman poet said, "I am a human being, therefore nothing human is foreign to me."

Surprising myself, I tell her what I'm going through, even the fantasies about my friend's handgun. She sucks in her breath, shows me her arm: goose bumps.

"I'm no longer there," I tell her. "Those thoughts passed."

She gives me a long and tight hug.

The thoughts startled me when they came. I'd worked through things and figured that they were long behind me. But perhaps suicidal thoughts are no different than an addiction. You can leave it behind, but if you trip into a dumpster full of drugs, temptation will rear its head.

The solution is to create new grooves so powerful that even if old patterns emerge, they are weakened. They don't last long. And the new grooves make sure you don't stick that damn needle in.

LVII

I spend time with Barb, Matt's practice manager. She's a wise woman who's had multiple organ transplants and beat every doctor's prediction to live an active and healthy life. She's also a qigong practitioner and offers me a session. I take it. One who loves himself accepts the help offered.

I lie on a massage table while she works on me. I close my eyes, drift off. Somewhere in that space between sleep and wake, I feel like I've just died and I go to meet God. God is a bright light in a vast and empty space. I drift closer to the light.

"How was life?" God asks.

"Pretty good," I say. Then, "thank you." I mean it.

"Not good enough," God says.

The light turns into a shiny brick wall reaching up to the sky, blocking me further.

"Go live great," God says.

LVIII

Dreams have a way of illuminating just how deep the rabbit hole goes. After rug-flip day, I had the very first nightmare of my life. I was being tortured by an unknown executioner while people stood around and watched. I woke up gasping out loud: "How could this happen?"

If I was crafting this story as fiction, I'd label the dream as too dramatic.

"Naah," I'd tell myself as I edited it out, "definitely cliché."

But your subconscious meets you where you are at.

I used to be proud of the fact that I never had nightmares. So much for that. Looks like everyone has a point where their safety snaps. This heartbreak was mine.

But even in this web are strands of gold. I loved her. I really loved her.

One time I said to her: "I don't just love you today. I love you thirty years from today."

I loved her from the inside out. This, I knew to my core. Be proud of being a man who can love his woman so deeply.

I slowly wake and tell Barb that I died in my dream.

"Then this is your rebirth," she says.

Dreams may show that you're falling. But they also show when you're on your way up.

LIX

It's night. I sit in the darkened living room and stare out the window. Oakland sparkles across the Bay. Most nights, container ships slide by, lit up like Christmas trees. Tonight, there is no movement.

I place my hand on my heart and say to myself softly: *I love you. I love you. I love you. I love you.*

I am speaking to myself, of course, but there is another layer. The current me is speaking to a younger me.

I did an exercise long ago where I imagined going back to the child who was molested. In one version, I saved him and ripped the molester's head off. Literally. In another, I went to the child who was hiding in shame and held him and promised him that I'd protect him.

I did various versions, but in each, it was the man that I became returning to save the child. In essence, saying to him, "I got you. I won't let anyone hurt you."

I did this with other parts of my childhood, other memories. All such exercises help. But I've learned that they are not one-offs, fixed and done with. The psyche is just too nuanced.

I need to reinforce whatever healing I experience. Make it a consistent practice. Or, better yet, fold it all into one practice that covers everything. And that is love.

LX

There is something I need to do that I've been putting off. That's okay, because I was in survival mode. Like the body shifting blood from extremities to vital organs. But to move to the next level, I must do this: forgive myself.

For all the ways I failed, for all the ways I could have been better, for all the mistakes I made, for all that I am holding against myself. Time to drop the weight, let it go.

So, I do. I grab a notebook and write down sentence by sentence whatever comes. Each I start with, "I forgive myself for . . ." I do this until there's nothing left. Then, I read it out loud to myself several times, feeling the weight of what I've been carrying.

Finished, I lace up my boots and head down to the Marina Green. There, I sit on the steps leading down to the water and add to the list. What surprises me is that more than just what I've been holding against myself from recent events comes up. Turns out, there was a deeper layer. But I had to go through this to discover it.

I finish with these sentences: "I forgive myself because I love myself. I forgive myself because I deserve love and joy and compassion and a magnificent life. I forgive myself because life loves me."

I read the whole thing out loud until something inside shifts and I know I'm done. I tear the sheet out. Then, I hop down to the rocks, find one that catches my eye, and wrap the paper around it with an eyeshade from a flight. The whole package feels hefty and solid in my hands.

I stare out at the Bay. Golden Gate bridge to the left, Alcatraz to the right. The infamous prison island glows under the setting sun. But the greatest prison ever created wasn't built with stone and cement. It's the mind.

I fling the package out to the water, watch it plop, and it's gone. Just gone. Then, I do the ten breaths. But instead of the usual, I say "thank you" with each breath and feel light naturally enter from above. Something has shifted. Rather than trying to make the light enter, I'm receiving it.

I walk away, boots stomping on the sidewalk with purpose.

LXI

I'll have to do this exercise in the future many times. The nature of being human means that I'll most likely fall short of who I can be. But that's okay. The more I love myself, the less gunk I'll accumulate. The less I'll have to let go of.

Think of yourself as a shoot that breaks through the earth and rises up, then plateaus. Then rises and eventually plateaus again. The pattern repeats. It's through loving yourself that you rise. It's through forgiving yourself that you overcome the plateaus. You grow and improve, inching closer to the light. To the greatest you.

LXII

Outside the gym, I call a friend in New York. Last time we spoke was the day after rug flip. I fill him in on what I've been up to, this obsessive focus on loving myself.

"It's wild," he says. "You seem so different. How long has it been?"

I have to think hard. Feels like a lifetime ago. "Three-ish weeks."

"Your voice is different," he says. "It's like you're powerful or something."

"That's funny," I say. "Power is a word that's been a focus lately."

"Talking to you," he says, "it's like you're radiating it."

I wouldn't go that far, but it's a nice thought.

"It's still hard, man. Just day by day."

"Hmm," he says, then is quiet for a moment. "If you'd been like this when she pulled that on you, what would you have done?"

I don't even have to think.

"I'd tell her that I deserve better and that we should work it out together. Because we still love each other. We owe what we have that. But if she didn't want to, then I'd let her go. With love. I'm an amazing man and her choice is her thing. Not mine."

My turn to be quiet.

"And I sure wouldn't have let it create or trigger insecurities. I'd focus on who I am and just be that."

"It sounds powerful to me," he says.

"I feel like I've been slapped awake," I tell him. "Like all this gunk's been ripped off. My headaches are gone. I'm being proactive about my health, doing whatever it takes, and I'm getting better fast. I can feel it in my body."

"That is loving yourself," he says.

I get off the phone and watch traffic go by. Yes, I'm loving myself. Yes, I'm starting to feel my power. And it all feels good. But it's tinged with sadness. I miss the way she'd relax into my arms when I held her. I miss those simple moments of loving her. And her loving me.

I let the missing wash over me. Letting myself feel is also loving myself. Then I walk into the gym and give the weights all I've got.

LXIII

I wake up with the thought, *I wonder what good I will experience today?*

It rises from nowhere. Just a gentle knowing that this is how life is becoming for me.

LXIV

What made this whole thing harder was that I didn't see it coming.

Maybe she told me and I didn't listen. Or she just blew a fuse. Or maybe it really did come out of nowhere. Whatever it was, that's that, and here I am, another morning, staring out the window at the Bay.

Gray clouds moving fast, the water an almost bluish green. Masts of moored sailboats swing hard in the wind. I think of death again, the greatest break. One that many never see coming. Yet there he is, clear as day, standing in front of me, awaiting my next breath.

Perhaps death is the greatest gift I have in my life. Each moment I step forward, he steps back. I never know which will be the last. Yet, I live like I have miles to go when in reality, I might only have inches left.

I don't need to be slapped awake again and again. I just have to stare death in his sockets and step forward with purpose, knowing that the next one isn't guaranteed.

Live this way and I won't have any choice but to be the greatest me.

LXV

I lie on the sofa and listen to a Wayne Dyer talk on YouTube. He was a friend of Cheryl and they often headlined conferences together.

"If you are what you think about," he says, "then you have to get real careful what you think about."

I like the firm conviction of truth in his voice.

"If you want to attract what's good in your life, but you're talking about what's missing and you're thinking about what's missing, you will continue to expand what's missing."

He definitely has my attention.

"I never talk about what's missing in my life. I only put my attention on what I intend to create."

I sit up. He just unlocked the next level.

"Whatever it is you want to attract into your life, say to yourself, 'it's on its way.' Four words. Just get them tattooed inside of your eyelids."

Then, he says something I fall in love with.

"Why have any of us learned to say, 'with my luck,' and having it mean that things aren't going to work out? Why wouldn't you say and have it as your habit: 'with my luck, it'll probably show up faster than it normally does'?

"Here's what happens: as you begin to shift the way you think, you can only act upon your thoughts. And as you start acting upon that thought, you start to become a collaborator with fate."

He just nailed how I've been feeling lately. That life is working for my good. Waypoint two on Tabreez's map.

After the video ends, I feel like even though Wayne passed away a few years ago, he just spoke directly to me. That's the beauty of the modern age. The wisdom and maps of others are available to us. Living them, that's our choice.

LXVI

I'm in the bathroom, getting ready for bed. I stare at myself in the mirror and lean in close. An intense love

rises inside. *Wow*, I think, looking into my eyes. *Wow.*
They are so beautiful. As is the man who stares through
them. How could I have forgotten?

The love for myself flows. There is no trying, no having to
repeat anything. It just flows.

LXVII

And, as if my mind has a grand sense of humor, I devolve
the next day. The missing rips through me hard. I walk
around, barely able to keep it together. The ten breaths
are like rolling boulders uphill. But I manage to ask
myself: *What would The Rock do?*

He'd go have a full-on workout. So I do. At least I'm
taking care of my body. Thank you, Mr. Rock.

I return to the apartment and meditate. Near the end, as
the music's ending, a voice deep within me says, *You're*
going to come through this fantastic. The thought feels
true. Something inside me relaxes.

If I was smart, I'd stay in that place. I'd make it last as long
as I could. I'd repeat the ten breaths. Instead, I call and
leave her a message.

"It's been a hard day," I say, "and I just needed to connect with you."

My voice starts to crack.

"I just wish . . . what I would give to return home—our home—and you'd be there and I'd put my head by your heart. Home."

I used to place my ear on her chest, listen to her heart. It was home. I feel like it's been ripped away.

"Your heart," I say. "My home."

I'm sobbing. It's not pretty.

"Moment of weakness," I say. "Moment of weakness."

Afterward, I stand there for a long time. I was planning on going out to see a friend, but something inside me says, *No, be in this space. Feel it. Tonight is too important.*

So rather than distracting myself, I stay in. I walk around the apartment, I stare out the windows, I do the ten breaths. No longer boulders, but still rocks. I'm tired of this suffering. I'm done.

And then, I know what I must do.

LXVIII

I grab a notebook, turn it sideways, and write hard into the paper:

> *I vow to love myself with everything I've got, in my thoughts, my actions, my words—because I am worthy of deep and full-on love.*

I date it. Then, I read it out loud ten times. By the fifth, something inside starts to shift. I'm carving these words into my mind.

I will read this out loud each morning, then live it. And if I stumble during the day, I'll read it aloud again with a ferocious intensity. Because that is what this vow deserves. Because that is what I deserve.

LXIX

Pain is like a catapult, it launches me. The direction it takes me, that's my choice. But just like a projectile, I will eventually run out of energy and slow down. Pain can only take me so far.

I need something that will pull me, not push. And as long as I give it what I got, it will return in kind. That's a vow.

A vow to oneself is a pure and sacred act. As I stare at mine, the pen still lying across the page, I feel like a dent was just made in the Universe. This is power.

LXX

Less than a half hour after I declare my vow, she calls me. There's a lot said about love on both sides. I cry. But nothing's changed. She's where she is and I'm where I am.

After the call ends, I stare at my vow. Something's bugging me.

She said to me: "I think you love me more than I love you."

That statement rings through my mind until I'm disgusted with myself. I need to put myself first. That vow will make sure I do.

I go and take a long cold shower. When I return to the living room, I look out at the darkness beyond the windows, and then I get on my knees. I'm not exactly the praying kind, but here I am.

"God," I say, "Bigger Than Me, life . . . I need to give this over to you."

I pause for a moment, searching deep inside. What arises surprises me a little, but the heart is what it is.

"My desire is that she and I are together, joyfully. And we have a beautiful life together. That is what I want. And I give it over to you."

So I do. And a weight lifts from my shoulders. Whatever results from this, I am okay with it. From this moment forward, I will only have one focus: keeping my vow.

LXXI

Last year, a company I was advising got sold. I'd told the founders to wait. They finally had traction in the market and their revenues were increasing month over month. They just had to keep doing what they were and they would build a company of a lifetime. Worst case, they could sell for significantly more than the current lowball offer.

But they sold. Months later, the CEO called and said that I was right. There's no harm in selling and taking cash off the table, everyone made money, but this shows the difference between good and great.

Good cashes out when things are decent. Great is patient and disciplined. It doesn't settle for decent and powers on forward. Entrepreneurship is full of such examples, individuals starting with zero and building massive companies. They all have one thing in common: founders with vision.

This morning, while reading my vow aloud, I realize that a vow is a vision as well. There is no compromise in a vow, you're all in. And if you fall, it gives you something to get up for. You stand and dust yourself off, then return to it. Your vow leads you to greatness.

LXXII

Giving it over doesn't mean giving up. I'm just handing over the weight of my desires to something Bigger Than Me. And remarkably, the act itself settles that needing feeling inside.

A butterfly flutters its wings in a rainforest, resulting in a tsunami halfway across the world. Life is so much more expansive than my mind can comprehend. I must trust in this. It will provide for me in ways greater than I could have imagined.

LXXIII

I walk over to where I did the forgiveness exercise. It's a cloudy evening, the parking lot still damp from the afternoon's rain, and the sun has already set. I do my sprints. In my rest time, I repeat successions of the loving myself breaths.

Finished, I sit on the high tide wall and listen to waves crash against rocks below. No sign of what I let go of just a few days ago. Life took it from me. I think of other things I'm holding against myself, and I open my palms and feel them drop. All so simple.

The evening grows darker. Joggers run by with flashlights. When I think of her and the missing arises, I open my palms again, wide, and give it over to Greater Than Me. So much better than the needless chatter in my head.

I think of Wayne Dyer's quote and laugh, saying to myself, *With my luck, magic will come faster than I imagined.* It feels good to think this. It feels real.

And why not? Whatever I believe is the filter that life shines through. It's up to me to choose one that makes me smile from the inside out.

LXXIV

A friend messages me. He's an ex-pat living in Bali.

"My girlfriend has a Theta healer slash therapist," he says. "She says she's amazing. I'd like to gift you a session."

I have no idea what a Theta whatchamacallit is, but I don't care. When life sends a gift, you accept.

"It's a little out there," he says. "Are you okay with that?"

I spent enough of my life in Northern California. Bring on the woo-woo.

Next thing I know, I'm in a Skype session with a blond Swedish woman named Erika in Ubud. She has a centered presence about her, warm and caring. It's like she glows.

Okay, worst case, I get to talk to a nice glowy person.

She walks me through her process, asking a series of questions about my beliefs, and something pops out.

"They always leave me," I find myself saying. "Anytime I love a woman deeply, she leaves me."

I can't believe what's coming out, but it fits. This has been a pattern as far as I can remember.

"And her," I say. "I loved her. It was real in every way. And she loved me. I would have bet everything that this wouldn't have happened."

I tell Erika about the time my mother left when I was a child. My father's beatings had gotten worse and she couldn't take it anymore. What it felt like to not be able to touch her. But this was something I thought I'd resolved already.

Besides, my mother returned, so why this pattern?

Erika guides me through other points in my life. My father, the molester, early relationships, and in all of them, that same belief snaking itself tighter.

I want to throw up. If that's my filter, any surprise how my life's played out?

"I'm so tired of this," I say.

"Good," she says, smiling. "It's time to let it go."

She does her Theta work, and you know what, I actually feel myself release it. It just goes. Poof. Afterward, we work on a new belief. I think through my list and decide upon this: I am a magnificent man and the woman I love loves me deeply and stays with me and we have a fantastic life together.

Then, I talk about her. Through all of this, through all the letting go, I still love her.

"She said she's going through something," I say. "That it's not about me."

Erika closes her eyes, is quiet for a long time.

"Then believe her," she finally says.

Before, it seemed impossible. My insecurities were running the show. But loving myself has weakened them.

"Okay." I nod. "And I love her, no matter what. I must let my heart be what it is."

A couple days later, my friend messages me: "my girlfriend bumped into Erika at the supermarket and Erika said that you inspired her."

I take it in and believe it. The old me who used to downplay compliments is gone. I accept the gifts that life offers. Then, I pull out my list and add to it: I inspire healers.

LXXV

It's night. I'm curled up on the sofa, watching sheets of rain under streetlamps. A container ship quietly glides through the bay, crosses under the bridge, and heads out to the open Pacific.

I haven't watched TV, read the news, or checked out what's happening on social media for almost a month. I could have lost myself in all sorts of distractions. But instead, I faced the fire and worked on my mind and body. I gave my all to my writing, to creating something special through this experience.

The man who comes through this will be far better than the one who went in.

That is loving myself.

LXXVI

Another difficult day. Missing feels like a gaping hole in my chest. I grab an Uber to see Matt for follow-up work. The driver doesn't look at me directly, and then I realize he has burn marks across his face and on his hands.

It's an hour's drive and gives me time to lose myself in thought. I do the ten breaths, but more in survival mode. As the car winds down Highway 280, I eye the driver's hands on the steering wheel.

Everyone's got scars. Whether outside or inside, they're there. Focusing on mine keeps me in darkness. It rewires old patterns. I think of Wayne Dyer only thinking about what he wanted to create. That's focusing on the light.

At Matt's office, Lisa draws my blood. When she's done, she puts her hand on my shoulder, squeezes it tight. The way she smiles, she must have sensed that I needed it.

Life is giving me love, always. And I accept it.

LXXVII

Let's be honest. I coasted for a long while. Meditating only when it was convenient or when I got around to it. When was the last time before rug flip that I loved myself consistently?

Life was going good, I got lazy, and then I had the injury and focused on what was wrong rather than what worked. What did I expect? The mind is plastic, no different than the body. Quit exercising for a year and live on doughnuts, see what happens.

I cashed out at decent when I should have continued to great. I must take responsibility for this. And whether I like it or not, I've been shaken awake. I must use this. There will be tough days again, I cannot let them slide me back.

I've already made my vow. I already know how to apply it. The next step is to create a series of rituals that make me do it consistently. Like brushing my teeth. So that no matter the storms, I always move forward.

LXXVIII

Observe a man's mind and you have a bird's-eye view to his destiny. Everything starts from within. Therefore, it's crucial to create habits of the mind.

I write down what I'll do daily to keep my vow. Upon waking, ten breaths. Then, coffee and read vow aloud, then meditate. In shower, ten breaths. Whenever walking or idle, ten breaths. At the gym, resting between sets, ten breaths. Before bed, looking into eyes in mirror and saying, "I love myself" until something shifts inside. In bed, falling asleep, ten breaths.

Lots to remember? Not really. There's a pattern here of intensity after waking and before sleep. Then, during the day, whenever the mind is idle, ten breaths. Simple.

This is my line in the sand. The bare minimum to keep my vow. So even if there are rough days, I'll continue deepening the grooves. Because I am worth it.

LXXIX

I once read a book where the author mentioned that he'd been able to get whatever he wanted by using affirmations. Each day, he'd write down fifteen times, "I, name, will . . ." and then state what he wanted. He was an extremely rational guy, trying this out of curiosity, and once it worked, he just used it.

He had nothing to sell. This wasn't what the book was about, in fact, it was almost an afterthought. He was sheepish about it, more sharing because, well, once you discover a truth that works, that's what you should do.

He tried rationalizing it, saying that affirmations focused the mind on what to pay attention to. A reasonable explanation. But he also said that many things he used this for were out of his control, and yet, they came.

I met him and, over dinner and drinks, asked him about it. *"All true,"* he said. In person, he gave no rationalization. He'd come to believe that they tapped into some fabric of reality that couldn't be explained.

Makes sense. We can rationalize our lives away, but deep down, we yearn for what is bigger. To flow with it. And when we find a way to do it, even if we never share it out of fear of ridicule, it comforts us. There are no atheists in foxholes under heavy bombardment.

So, all this repetition of loving myself, is it just an affirmation? Maybe. Is it a rewiring of neural pathways in my brain? After all, it's well known that neurons that fire together wire together. The more you fire and wire them, the stronger the pathway, and the more it fires on its own. Sure. Reasonable explanation.

But does this explain the shifts that are happening in my life? The opportunities popping up, things I didn't know how to make happen naturally happening on their own? Maybe. I could take each, break it down, and rationalize it away.

But does that serve me? My belief is the magnifying glass that life shines through.

The maps and beliefs of humanity are available to me. I must pick what speaks to me, then go all in. Life rewards me when I take a stand, when I say, "This is what I believe in and I'm going to live it fully."

Not when I coast. That's a truth I've learned.

LXXX

I hit the gym. Already, I'm in the best shape I've been in years. My diet is on point, no exceptions. Whenever I'm tempted to cheat or slide, I ask myself, *If I loved myself, what would I do?* The answer is clear and I live it.

Each time I live the answer, I reinforce the pathway of making loving choices for myself. I used to do this before, but I'm on a whole different level. That's what happens when you do everything to keep your vow.

Watch your mind sometime and you'll realize that it's always answering questions. Fear is an answer to what could go wrong. Pain is an answer to what's missing. You'll quickly realize that the mind naturally goes for the negative, not the light.

So you must consciously ask yourself empowering questions. Ones that result in you making loving choices for yourself. Do this for a while, and you'll need to ask them less. Living the answers will have become habit.

LXXXI

Years ago, over dinner, a friend told me that she'd died and was brought back. Clinically dead for eight minutes, the real thing. I had to ask.

"Did anything happen . . . while you were, you know?"

She shook her head. She didn't remember a thing. Then, she glanced around, put her fork down, and whispered: "What if this is heaven?"

She leaned back and watched me.

"I died," she said. "How do I know that this isn't the other side?"

It was one of those moments where time stood still. I felt like someone'd just bonked me on the head. Neither of us spoke for a while.

"So that's how I live," she finally said. "Like this is heaven."

One heck of a belief.

LXXXII

I stop by Matt's office. He's out of town, but I'm getting an IV with vitamins and all sorts of good stuff. Why? Self-care is loving yourself.

Lisa walks into the room to put in my IV.

"Oh, those are so pretty," she says, staring at the flowers by the window.

She fluffs up a warming pad, places it under my arms, then gently inserts the needle in my hand. She tells me that she took Zumba this morning, which made her feel good all day.

Then her face goes soft. Her son used to work out in that gym. Sometimes when she took classes, she'd watch him exercise through the glass wall.

"People say that I should cut down," she says. "I've got pictures of him everywhere, on my phone. But I don't want to. He's a part of me."

She clips the tube to the needle, gets the fluid going, then wraps my hand with a red bandage. Finished, she sighs.

"But I suppose I should . . ."

Would she say that this was heaven? I don't ask.

Here she is, still appreciating moments of beauty in the day, smiling to her patients, taking care of them in her gentle and loving way. Creating little slices of heaven with her presence.

"I almost got a tattoo this week," she says. "Didn't happen, but I will. What do you think: name on my wrist or a bird?"

"Bird," I say. "A symbol's better."

I tell her about my favorite symbol, the lotus. Rising through the muck, opening to the light.

She smiles. "Symbol it is."

She gathers the waste and leaves. I think about my symbol again. A lotus doesn't force itself to open to receive the light, it's the other way around. The light opens it.

All the work I'm doing to love myself, there must be a level above. Where there is no effort, no fighting against resistance. Just allowing myself to receive the love that was mine all along.

LXXXIII

So I do it. In bed at night, I repeat the ten breaths until I fall asleep. But this time, there is no forcing. I breathe deeper, slower, feeling love enter. No resistance, just receiving what is mine.

I wake up smiling. Then, I immediately turn to the ten breaths. Receiving my love, receiving the light.

LXXXIV

Why ten breaths? Because it's easy to remember. Large enough that it causes a slight shift each time. Small enough to bypass any excuse.

Most importantly, it keeps you consistent to your commitment to love yourself. But this doesn't mean that you do a few ten breaths a day and you're good to go. It is the bare minimum. The more you give of yourself, the more you receive.

In fact, do stretches of ten minutes of nonstop ten breaths. Replace something that would have filled your time but not contributed to your well-being with this. It's your healing. It's your life. Give yourself the attention you deserve.

LXXXV

Nighttime is perfect for the ten-minute stretches of ten breaths. I'm in bed, winding down the day, so it's easier to layer love into my subconsciousness. I set a timer. Then, with each in-breath, I expand my chest and allow love and light to enter. When I breathe out, I let go of whatever goes. That's it.

Sometimes, I repeat "I love myself" with the in-breath. Sometimes, I don't. But with each, I let myself feel it. That's turning out to be the most important part. Feeling.

This is also a great way to remove the gunk and emotional charge built up over the day. Better to drop it here than carry the weight into tomorrow.

LXXXVI

In two days, I'll fly to New York. I imagine the apartment
I'll walk into, her things gone. The closets empty. I
wonder what it'll feel like, but who knows. All I know
is that no matter what, I am a magnificent man who's
started loving himself again.

That is going to be another starting point. I will fiercely
love myself from there.

LXXXVII

I stop by Matt's office again. I fly out tomorrow
morning. When I see Lisa, I give her the gift I brought.
It's a light device I recently bought to stimulate vitamin
D production. Last week, she mentioned that she'd
borrowed a unit and it made her feel good and she was
saving up to buy one.

"Are you sure," she says, almost hugging it. "Can't I pay
you something?"

"It's a gift," I say. "The point is to accept it."

"It's easier for me to give," she says. "Not to receive."

"That's why you should receive even more."

I'm being myself again. Smiling more. Giving. I'm better in so many ways than just a month ago. My heart still hurts, but a heart that loves this deeply will feel both ways. There's a beauty in that, too.

I'm still in the early stages, I know that. The longer I love myself, the more the effects compound. But still, could my progress have been faster?

Honestly, yes. I should have taken my own advice. It would have led me to forgiving myself and making my vow immediately. There is something special about those acts. Life shifts in your favor the moment you do them.

But I'd coasted for too long. No surprise then that I got caught up in my head, in what had gone wrong, rather than what I knew to do. The mind is tricky that way. Left to its own devices, it will put what we need the most last.

That's okay. I forgive myself for that, too. That's loving myself.

LXXXVIII

So how does this whole thing work? Do you decide to love yourself and then winning lottery tickets rain down from above and you never have another care in the world? It's more beautiful and nuanced than that. Things do start to work. Experiences and resources out of your reach find you. I've seen it happen again and again.

But you have to step up to them. You have to go where they take you. And if ever confused about what to do, just ask if you're taking action from love or fear. Make it love, always.

Another thing that happens is that you get internal nudges. Often in meditation. Things to do, people to reach out to, what to say. Listen to these. This is life guiding you.

You also get honest and real in your interactions. Your mind is too important to distract itself with conversations full of nothing. You find yourself expressing things that you thought for years but held back, afraid of how the other might take it. You do this with kindness. Don't be surprised if it sometimes creates conflict. But interestingly, it raises your relationships to a whole different level.

Along with this realness comes greater discernment about who you allow in your life. You're clear with yourself about their intentions. No justifications, no projections. Zero excuses. Because eventually, those intentions will catch up with you. Your life is too important for poor intentions.

Many of your fears naturally lessen. After all, they're just old mental loops. You start to see through the hallucinated snakes. And when confused, you ask yourself if the thought rose from love or fear. That resolves that.

The greatest shift: you start letting go. What you held against yourself, what you held against others. The guilt, the shame, the pain. The needless suffering. As you drop the weight, you realize the truth—illusions of the mind, all. What is left is you, reborn, giving yourself love. You live from this place.

Lastly, you find yourself having moments of gratitude. Sometimes they rise out of nowhere. Sometimes from the way that life is unfolding for you.

Do you achieve perfection? Not if you're human. But you are vastly better than before. How do you know for sure? Simple, just observe your thoughts. And since your thoughts determine your destiny, your reality shifts to reflect them.

Hippocrates said, let food be thy medicine and medicine be thy food. Tweak it to this: Let thoughts be thy medicine and medicine be thy thoughts.

LXXXIX

If I were to boil this down for you, what would I say?

I'd say: don't wait until you need to. Start this very moment. Go all in on loving yourself.

First, forgive yourself. This wipes the slate clean. Next, make the vow. It is a declaration to yourself and life on who you'll be. The act itself is a defining moment. Then, do everything it takes to keep it. Step up to love, and life will step up in return.

I'd also say: don't coast. No matter how good it gets, no matter what excuses the mind creates, don't coast. Go all in again and again.

Then, I'd say one more thing: share what you learn from this. In sharing your experience, you are better, and the world is better. It's that simple.

XC

Rainy morning in San Francisco. Bags packed, the place clean. It's time to head to the airport. I fill my cup with water and walk to the plants one last time. What I see makes me grin. In the large one, among the dead-looking branches, rise two beautiful bright green leaves. Both from the same spot, like the unfolding of a heart.

I stand there for a while, admiring them. When you give love, life returns.

FROM KAMAL

If you found this book helpful, please review and share it.
That helps it find its way to those who need it. This would
mean a lot to me. Thank you.

And please feel free to email me at k@founderzen.com.